Modern Shamans

By clearing your thoughts and emotions

of old programs

you discover the joy of living free.

Nancy DeYoung

MODERN SHAMANS

by Nancy DeYoung

Copyright © 2007 by Nancy DeYoung

Original drawings by Alexandria Z. Noble

Published in the United States by

Nancy DeYoung

www.ndeyoung.com

ISBN 978-0-6151-4222-7

Printed in the United States of America

Acknowledgements

This book would not be possible if it had not been for Vickie, my friend and mentor. Her willingness to teach others and myself what she knows about etheric clearing paved the way for me to do this work and eventually write this book.

Many thanks go to my dear friend Peggy for lovingly nudging me to contact Vickie to experience an etheric clearing.

Without the help of Klaus, Nina, Donna and Pearlene this manuscript may never have appeared in readable form. I thank all my helpers for their time, patience, wonderful feedback and great editing skills.

My special thanks goes to Alexandria who has worked many hours by my side developing new techniques and energetically supporting me while writing this book. It was also her talent that created the magical illustrations in this book.

Barbara did an awesome job designing the cover art. She was given the photos one day and had the cover designed and back to me the next! My thanks also go to Gary, Pearlene, Gabrielle and Graham for their help at the photo shoot.

My appreciation goes to Donna and Harty whose support made it easier for me to focus on writing.

I acknowledge all friends, clients and class participants who taught me and provided the stories I have included in this book. Because of their experiences and willingness to move forward in their lives, we are all able to learn and benefit.

The meadowlark sings its song.

I too put my head back,

lift my face to the sun,

and give my song to the world.

Contents

Foreword
by P.M.H. Atwater, L.H.D

The term "shaman" is said to be a Tibetan word meaning "one who knows." What distinguishes shamanism from other forms of knowing is that practitioners of the artform "journey" to non-ordinary states of consciousness both within the self and throughout the "luminous energy matrix" that undergirds all creation and all created things. They seek for learning, for guidance, for knowledge, for direction, for the power to heal in service to others, their community, themselves.

Shamanism is not a game, nor is it a system of techniques or another "new age" gimmick. It is a journey into nothing (no-thing) where endings are revealed and the mystery of mysteries is laid bare. It is a journey into spirit in the company of spirts, to reach in and beyond that which is "spiritual." Shamanism is as old as the First Peoples and as young as babes of the 21st century ... forever relevant. My childhood arranged itself around this truth, unveiling an energy matrix more real than fingers and toes, more touchable and lively than what I was later taught to regard as "physical." Then I met the Spirit Keepers.

It was a bright Saturday. I may have been 10, perhaps 11, when the high pasture near the rim of Rock Creek Canyon south of Twin Falls, Idaho, became my refuge. Hatred oozed from each step as I screamed at the injustices and cruelty of my life, of a mother who never mothered me, of another mother who did yet we were kept apart, of a parade of men each answering to the title "father" who convinced me they were no such thing. I sat on a log to moan my fate.

Suddenly, from the grasses, soil, and rocks there arose the energy that resided within each of those forms, the energy that enabled the natural world to exist. This energy lifted as if "mountains" were oozing upward from the earth to create large and small peaks; all around me, peaks, I could see through and feel through. I imagined on each peak a face yet there were none, no features, just glistening, shimmering mini-mountains of purest energy. We spoke, though not in words so much as feelings, senses, images, sounds, rhythms, pulsations. They called themselves Spirit Keepers and impressed upon me that it was their job to hold together spirit and matter, like "glue," so Creation could manifest. They showed me how each area on the planet had Spirit Keepers to maintain the flow of The Great Breath as It breathed through Its own thoughts ... Creation assured.

I learned more from the Spirit Keepers than I did from school. They taught me things like how to merge into rock and soil, become whatever I focused on, how to release what twisted my soul. They were my friends and we shared many mo-ments. For years afterward I encountered them wherever I went. After I died three times in three months in 1977, and each time had a near-death experience, I walked out on my life and journeyed east, settling down in the state of Virginia.

Part of my healing journey into wholeness was a par-ticular evening when I encountered the Spirit Keepers of the Shenandoah River and came to realize that I, too, was a Spirit Keeper. We all are. As we awaken to other worlds and greater realities, as we peer through the veils that sepa-rate perception from fact, we become as if acupuncture needles in how our energy, the sum of us, steadies and nourishes the earth and all therein with each step we take, each breath we breathe.

Part of everyone's journey into wholeness is reaching that place in knowing where we can accept our call to serve the healing of self, others, our world. Shamans, once they move through the artforms of knowing that they know, be-come invaluable servers who quietly and dependably re-store balance as they reconnect the head with the heart.

This is where Nancy DeYoung shines. She takes the alchemical process of clearing and cleaning subtle-body energy and turns it into practical, usable measures anyone can use to heal self and others. She speaks with a voice that is direct and practical, that unites the sensitivities of tradition with the demands of our modern world and the tension we all feel in these rapidly changing times. I never imagined that a do-it-yourself manual would be possible in shamanism. Here it is: not so much in explaining what really cannot be explained, but rather in application, how to become what a shaman really is ... a healer who serves.

Congratulations, Nancy. Job well done.

Various self-published books and e-books by P.M.H. Atwater, L.D.H. are available on her website:

http://www.pmhatwater.com

Columns written for newsletters and websites, are archived on her blog:

http://pmhatwater.blogspot.com

A list of her books appears at the end of this book following the "Recommended Reading" section.

Introduction

*If we do not define ourselves for ourselves,
we will be defined by others—for their use
and our detriment.*

Audre Lorde

Modern Shamans takes you on a journey outside time and space where you can quickly and easily claim the power that is rightfully yours. This book shows you how to combine the truths the shamans have known with simple principles of quantum physics creating an alchemical process to change thoughts and clear emotions. As you claim responsibility and step into your power, you become the modern shaman.

The chapters in *Modern Shamans* begin with information on a particular subject. The chapters close with an exercise designed to help you understand and integrate the information. This book may challenge some of your beliefs. As you read it and work through the exercises, I ask that you keep an open mind and just see where it takes you. I can't prove that any of the material in this book will work for you, but you can prove it for yourself.

You can read this book for the information only. You can read the book and do some of the exercises. Or you can work your way through it fully, with the intention of making a difference in your life. Your results will be determined by the intent you hold and how much change you really want to bring into your life.

Modern Shamans is a book of tools that can be used or stored on the bookshelf. Stored tools aren't worth much, but whatever the depth of your involvement, you will benefit by being open to these alchemical ways of moving forward in life. They are alchemical because of the transformational power that comes from recognizing you are not a victim of circumstances, but rather a perfectly complete being capable of creating anything you desire.

Responsibility

It has become necessary for us to take more responsibility for our own health because the medical profession has fallen short in helping us maintain a state of well-being. Once we are sick they treat the disease, but wouldn't it be better to prevent disease? While this book will help you help yourself, there may be times when it is necessary for you to receive help from a medical doctor or health practitioner; those times are for you to determine. This book is not a substitute for medical treatment. It was written to provide techniques and suggestions you can use to help yourself, a guide to show how body, mind, emotions, and spirit work together.

You can use this book as a roadmap to remembering wholeness. In our true state, we are and always have been whole and one with all. We are not broken nor do we need to be fixed, but we have played roles that have caused us to believe that this is the case. The information and techniques in this book help clear the fog so we can recognize truth.

Before we start, I state this book is my truth as I see it at this time. Tomorrow my truth may be different. I ask that you and your high self determine what is true for you and that each time you pick up this book you ask for discernment in interpreting and using this information. This frees me to tell you my experiences. It also honors you.

The days of the shaman and guru as singular, specialized members of the tribe are coming to an end. It is time for all of us to become our own shaman and guru, accepting responsibility for ourselves and learning to work through and clear our own dramas. I encourage you to do as much of your own work as possible. If you reach a place where you get stuck and need help, then search out a practitioner to assist you.

Quick Fix, Plodding, or Alchemy

There are those who are looking for a quick fix or some fast, simple prescription by which to live. There are also those who feel a need to always be processing something, like a dog chewing on a bone. This book presents a different approach. It contains information on how to move from fragmentation into a healthy state of being at a safe and steady pace. There is no need to rush so fast you miss the good stuff nor to plod along slowly at a fearful pace. This book will help you clear blockages and work through situations in ways that are fun, effective, and empowering.

By working alchemically on the etheric level, you transmute your unhealthy thoughts, emotions, beliefs, programming, and judgments. When you realize things can change NOW and you make the choice to do so, your perceptions alter. The power your problems have over you diminishes. This brings change.

By this point in time, you have probably over-processed your life. As long as your attention is focused on healing yourself, you keep attracting more wounds that need to be healed. If instead you focus on growth, you will have more experiences that help you grow. The gift in this is that growth experiences are often more pleasant than healing experiences.

You don't have to process your stuff anymore. You only need to recognize that you are growing and you are in this life to gain experiences that help you expand. You can't do this if you keep relating to the hurts of your past because then you interpret your present based on past pain. You have a choice. How you look at life determines how you interpret your daily experiences. Will your memories be filled with wounds or opportunities?

Paradigm Shifts

The exercises in this book were designed to assist you in shifting your paradigms and claiming your power. The techniques can be used in privacy or with the help of a trusted friend. When choosing someone to work with, ask your heart who the right person for you is. The friend can read the exercises and be there for emotional support. If working alone, it may help to record the exercises on audio-tape and play them back while relaxing.

Every time you pick up this book or work with the exercises, ask that the light surround and protect you. Call in the beings working for your best and highest good and give

them permission to work with you. In this way you can receive energy while reading, even before you begin the exercises. Evoking this protection ensures that only those energies that serve the highest purpose will be present.

How the alchemy discussed in this book works may not
be easily explained to the logical mind. This, however, does
not decrease its effectiveness in clearing present-day health
issues, mending broken hearts, improving relationships, releasing addictions, and dissipating fear. When working with
alchemy, you can expect lightness, clarity, self-confidence,
and peace in your life. It works. So let us begin the journey
of the modern shaman into truth here and now—together.

Chapter 1
How I Became a Modern Shaman

Life is a precious gift. Don't waste it being unhappy, dissatisfied, or anything less than you can be.

Anonymous

The Trade

Vickie had horses, and in return for bodywork, I created a compost pile for her. I gathered up the dried horse manure from her field and sifted it through a screen into a fine powder, breaking up clods and removing the rocks, weeds and centipedes. When the fence was lined with piles of the filtered dust, we made a frame of boards and screens. We layered the aged manure with grass and straw. By fall it would be rich fertilizer to put back on the field.

I enjoyed the hours I spent in the warm sun with the gentle breeze blowing. It gave me time to think. I couldn't tell you what I thought about, it was the kind of thinking that you don't really notice—when thoughts just seem to

1

drift through, not stopping long enough to be recognized. This was a luxury after the years I had spent in the office tending to the many details of business operations.

I had left a successful job in Cleveland, Ohio, to move to Boulder, Colorado. After the move, I did some temp work in various offices and was offered a number of permanent positions, but it didn't feel right to take any of them. I was looking for something totally different, but I didn't know what it was. This is why I wanted an etheric clearing session with Vickie—I hoped she would be able to help me uncover what that "something" was.

When I did enough work to earn my first etheric clearing, I drove down the blacktop road leading into the country where Vickie lived. I pulled into the long driveway that led to the domed building where she worked. She was waiting for me.

I was nervous because I didn't know exactly what to expect. All I knew was that I was about to have an etheric clearing. When I asked what that meant I was told, "You just have to experience it; it is different for everybody." Basically I knew the word "etheric" meant that is was not of the earth. Webster had been no help. It said: "a hypothetical invisible substance postulated as pervading space and serving as the medium for the transmission of light waves and other forms of energy." So I surrendered to the process and decided I would know soon enough.

Vickie instructed me to lie face-up on the massage table. She said she would explain what she was seeing and doing as she worked. First she grounded herself and set up a protective field in which to work. She looked at my etheric bodies to see how each was feeling. From that she determined we needed to go back to when I was six years old, which was when my mother died. She said I had lost parts of my self and we needed to get them back.

My mother had four children spaced 18 months apart. I was the second oldest. My older sister was hardly ever home, though I am not sure where she was—school or my grandmother's house, I suspect. From the time I was three years old, my mother relied on me to help her tend the younger children, often leaving me with them while she drove my sister wherever it was she went. Since Mother frequently was sick, I also cared for her.

My grandmother told me that when my mother died, I sat on the sofa and stared out the window for three days. I would not eat or talk to anyone. I just sat there and stared. I do not remember this, but I do remember feeling empty inside. In the work I did with Vickie, I felt shame and abandonment. I had done the very best I could to care for my mother, but it wasn't enough to keep her alive. We found that when she died, I felt it was my fault—I had failed in my job. The family told me she had gone to live with Jesus. Why would she do that? Didn't she love me? Was it because I had failed her? It left the child part of me feeling hurt, abandoned, and responsible.

Vickie explained that my six-year-old self felt empty because a part of her had left with my mother. We asked for the pieces I had lost as a child and I saw her receive a crystal shard that was golden orange. It moved into the top of my head and turned to light and went through my body filling it with the happy light of childhood.

Because of the responsibility I had as a child, I had lost my childhood and was now getting it back. As it came in, a weight lifted from my heart and I felt lighter than I could ever remember. As I absorbed this piece into me, I vowed that I would continue sifting manure as long as I could in order to earn more of these wonderful etheric clearings. This was just the beginning of my many sessions with Vickie.

Every time we met, we delved into different issues, and I experienced immediate healing from each of them. We retrieved my fragments and I released things that didn't belong to me. She worked on my core and chakras (more on this later). The thing I liked about this work was that I always left feeling good, and once I released stuff, it didn't come back.

While I was doing this work with Vickie, my twenty-six-year-old daughter was going through traditional psychotherapy. As she worked on her issues with her father and me, she went through periods where she didn't want to talk to or be around me. The work she was doing was bringing her issues up, but was not giving her a way to release them. Since there was no resolution, she re-experienced the emotions all over again compounding the impact of the original situation. Her anger and moodiness made life difficult, since she was living with me and going to college.

How different the clearings were! Once I recalled an event and we cleared it, the energy of anger and pain were gone. After each clearing, I felt good (though sometimes tired) and I never experienced anger or resentment toward the person with whom we had done the clearing.

Needless to say, I spent the spring building a compost pile so I could earn more clearings. As I stood in the fresh air, listening to the bird's song, sifting manure, I realized how appropriate it was that I turn waste product into gold for Vickie's fields while she turned my old sludge into treasures for me. It was worth it, the process was easy and it worked.

A Taste of Energy

One day in August I went to my appointment with Vickie. When I arrived, she was on the telephone with her friend Alice. She hung up hurting from the argument they just had. I jokingly said maybe I should work on her. She closed her eyes and said, "Yes, you need to do that." Wow, I was only kidding. I was good at receiving the work, but didn't know anything about doing it for someone else, but I decided she could guide me through and it would be fun to experiment.

She lay down on the table and I stood beside it, as she had done for the last two months with me. I sent my root chakra (more on this later) into the earth to ground me. I called in the beings of light as she had done. I envisioned a tube of light surrounding us. As I did these things, I felt a surge of energy go through my body. Something was happening.

Once the space was ready to work in, she told me to place my hands side by side on her abdomen. As I did, a stream of energy coursed through my body, which continued the whole time we worked. I had never felt anything

like that before. I was so excited, but I re-centered myself
and tuned in to her energy to see what was causing her relationship with Alice to be so unpleasant. I saw a scene,
which explained what had happened. We retrieved her
pieces and cleared the energy that was not hers.

I was exhilarated and surprised at how easily the energy flowed through me and that I actually saw something.
I asked her to teach me more. She said she would, but I figured that was something she probably would never get
around to doing. The discussion ended, but the experience
was just beginning.

The Trigger

In December of that year, I gave myself a special birth-
day present. I went to Egypt for a healing conference, because I wanted to have a healing experience, not because I
thought I was a healer. The event with Vickie did not leave
me with any delusions about my abilities. In fact I have
never believed that anyone heals another. Instead, we help
the person accomplish it himself by providing information
or an extra boost of energy.

On the flight to New York I wrote down my goals for
the trip. I wanted to come home with clarity concerning my
life work and all the new information that had entered my

reality that last year. So much had happened I wasn't sure what I believed, and I wasn't sure what to do with what I did believe.

The tour group gathered in the international terminal of the airport in New York. I looked around, curious about who I would be spending the next ten days with. Most everyone appeared quite ordinary, but there was one lady who gave me shivers when I saw her. My first impulse was that she was handling very dark energies, but I shoved the feeling aside. Jackie who was my assigned roommate finally arrived and I felt comfortable with her right away.

After hours of waiting, the boarding call for our flight was announced. We were beginning the eleven-hour trip to Egypt. I sat next to a lady who slept most of the time, but I was too excited to sleep, so I wrote in my journal.

Somewhere over Spain, I wrote, "I ask that all this stuff and who I am be made known to me on this trip. I do not want to be in the dark anymore. I want to get off the fence and leave fear behind."

We landed at the Cairo Airport in the early morning hours. From some recess of my being, I recognized the smells, the people and the air as clearly as if I had been there yesterday. I felt I had returned home. We were shuffled through customs and on to the Hotel Oberi. My adventure was unfolding.

During the first few days, Jackie and I attended parts of the program. We usually had a late dinner and then went to our room and discussed the day's talks and events.

Each night the woman who had seemed so dark to me entered Jackie's dreams, trying to control her. I told her about the work I had done with Vickie. She was aware of subtle energies and felt brave enough to have me attempt working with her to resolve the issue with the woman.

We were scheduled to enter the Great Pyramid the next morning at 5:00. I had been sick all day with nausea, diarrhea and cramps. It was nothing I ate and I did not have the flu; it was simply a cleansing preparation for the experience I would have in the morning. Although I wasn't feeling well, we decided to attempt the clearing work. So I centered myself, called in the light beings, set up the tube of light and then looked to see what we needed to do.

The energy flowed through me into my new friend. After a while, the flow became uncomfortable for me. My hands were stinging as if they were freezing cold and then suddenly thrust into hot water. The feeling was spreading up my arms. I was going to be sick again and had to stop to go to the restroom. I lay down on the restroom floor trying to decide whether to put my head in or my bottom on the toilet. In that moment, the dark woman appeared to me. She asked what my intent was. I explained to her that I had no issues with her but that Jackie did not want to have a connection with her and had asked me to help her stop it. I further explained that I had no intention of doing battle with her. The apparition vanished.

When I told Jackie about the experience, we decided she had gotten what she needed, and that we were finished. This experience left me feeling tired, but ecstatic that something happened.

The next morning when we entered the Pyramid, the woman was there. She stood on the ledge outside the king's chamber staring down at us as we climbed the staircase. She did not enter with the group and we did not see her at any of the meetings for the remainder of the conference. Jackie had no more dream encounters with her.

Failed Initiation Re-experienced

We entered the Pyramid at 5:00 a.m. before it opened to the public. We were to have a private ceremony in the king's chamber, which would be led by Wallace Black Elk, a Native American elder. Before the ceremony began, we had time on our own to explore the Pyramid. As I entered the Pyramid, I felt something important was going to happen, but I didn't know what it was. It wasn't until later that I understood I would re-experience a test that at some point in my existence I had previously failed. I call this an initiation.

I put my backpack in a wall niche by the entrance. I was dehydrated from being sick. I had brought water, but there were no restrooms so I was afraid to drink it for fear of being sick again. I did not know the layout of the Pyramid, so I followed the group down a ramp. I didn't know where we were going. As I crawled the last few yards on my hands and knees into the chamber, tears filled my eyes. I found myself crying, "This time I will do it. Whatever it takes, this time I will do it." I did not know what IT was; I just knew I was not going to fail this time.

Panic was growing inside me. Sweat was pouring from me. It only increased as I stood up in the room. I felt lost and did not know how to get out. I tried to talk to several people on our tour, but they looked through me as if I wasn't even there and no one would answer. Why wouldn't they talk to me? It appeared they couldn't see me. I was terrified.

No one could help me—they couldn't even see me! I knew I had to calm myself, so I sat down and tried to figure things out. What was happening? Besides those of us I could see, there were others on the tour, where were they? I thought they must have been ahead of me and had gone out another exit, but when I searched, there weren't any other exits. What happened to them? I felt trapped.

I kept pushing the panic aside to make sense of what was happening. I did not understand, but decided I would leave the way I had entered. But now there was a woman sitting in the doorway wailing. Along with the panic I, too, was feeling tremendous grief. I sobbed with her. It was the pain of loss, of having failed. I allowed it to permeate my body. I felt I would burst. By recognizing it, something released inside of me, but I did not know what.

With this release came the knowledge that the others in the group had taken another route in the Pyramid and I had to return the way I had come. The feeling of loss was still with me but the fear was gone and I knew I was now free to leave this area of the Pyramid. As if on cue, the woman moved from the doorway and I passed through.

Failed Initiation Released

I climbed back up the ramp from the lower chamber. The lack of oxygen and strange combination of smells added to the nausea and weakness I felt. I was exhausted on all levels. I pulled my water bottle from the niche where I had stashed it and took a sip, only enough to wet my lips for I didn't want to be sick again.

Then I continued the climb to the queen's chamber. The entryway was low and I bent over as I entered the room. My head ached. I sat down on the floor in the corner to my right, feeling I had been there many times before. Sitting there, something shifted inside of me but I didn't know what. Peace entered my being. I wept profusely.

Initiation Completed

I climbed more steps to the king's chamber. As I entered, Wallace Black Elk was laying out rocks, feathers, tobacco and other sacred items in preparation for leading the ceremony. Exhausted I lay down on the floor and waited for it to begin.

The lights were turned out and we sat in total darkness. A voice, perhaps from the past, whispered in my head that it was time to stop mourning the past and to move on. The shame of letting others and myself down and the pain of failure could now be released. I felt totally drained, exhausted and relieved. There were no tears left to cry.

My vision became acute. Although we were in total darkness, I could see and feel each person. I saw flashes of light. Joy and gratitude flooded my heart. I did not feel elated, but calm, tired, and vulnerable. I had completed the initiation. After the ceremony, I went back to the hotel and slept for 22 hours.

Life After Initiation

I was relatively new to these kinds of experiences and most of what happened did not make much sense to me. I didn't realize at the time what a profound effect this trip would play in my life. I recorded in my journal on the flight home, "I do not feel that anything has happened to really change me on this trip. I did complete the initiation but what does that mean in terms of my life? I don't feel much different today."

It wasn't until later that the effects of completing the initiation became real to me. When I returned home, I moved out of a friend's basement into an apartment of my own. I realized something had been awakened inside of me. I begged Vickie to teach me everything she knew about etheric clearing. My pleading paid off and in January she taught her first class. I was on my way into a new life's work.

Bends in the Road

I worked four years with the techniques that Vickie taught me, sometimes adding to them, as I discovered new information. They were effective and the work benefited people more than any other method I was aware of, but I was ready for more. Then I met Alexandria.

We were attending a Global Sciences Congress in Denver. She was standing at a table looking at some herbal supplements. I had been talking to her friend Dennis and he pointed her out and told me I should go over and meet her. So I did. We connected instantly. We talked about the work we did and decided it would be fun to do a trade so we could experience each other's work. I was to go to her house in Louisville on Monday at 11:00 a.m.

To help her bridge to a new way of working, Alexandria learned the techniques I used. As we did clearings for each other, we experimented. We remained open and followed the guidance we received. We found that we could make modifications that sped up and amplified the results. By simplifying the clearing techniques, we were able to work on ourselves. Together Alexandria and I created an approach to clearing that surpassed anything either of us had previously experienced.

The next year, Alexandria moved to an island and I moved to New Mexico, so we no longer had each other to help us do our own work. We could do some of the work on our own, but sometimes we needed help. To continue working together, she suggested we do distance clearings. We tried and found they worked as well as if we were together; we didn't need to be physically with each other. This was possible because the work is done outside of time and space.

Later I led workshops in which I taught others what I had learned. We always did exercises in the groups to help the participants integrate what we discussed. They were simple techniques that could be taken home and repeated whenever needed. These exercises were based on the ones I had been using to work on myself. The members of the groups later reported on the wonderful experiences they had, saying the exercises were simple and yet they worked. Some of these techniques are recorded in this book, so you can also work with them.

Modern Shamans is my next step in the clearing work. I have reached many people through the workshops and on a one-to-one basis in private sessions and now it is time to pass on the information I have gathered since 1992 in book form. With this knowledge and the exercises, you can do the clearing work for yourself. If you do the exercises and feel nothing is happening, look at your life and yourself and see if there have been changes. That is where the real proof lies. If you see changes occurring there, know the work is effective even if you don't feel anything right now—in time you will.

The Future

You can take the work described here, and grow with it as you add your own experience to it. There is always another step to take in this journey beyond time and space.

Chapter 2
Creation

If you want to be happy, set a goal that commands your thoughts, liberates your energy and inspires your hopes.

Andrew Carnegie

The Way of Creation

The first step in becoming a modern shaman is to realize *who* the creator is. When I realized that *I* was the sole agent responsible for the creation of every aspect of my world, I realized I had the ability to change anything that wasn't to my liking.

> *We create our world.*
> *Our thoughts and emotions*
> *are the tools we use to create.*

Through thought and emotion, every part of your world is given existence. Decisions made knowingly lead to the circumstances in your life. Decisions you fail to make are made for you, thereby bringing about situations with which you have to contend. For example, ignore maintenance items in your car and the car is liable to break down.

It may not seem that you have created everything that is happening to you, especially if it is less than pleasing. You may be thinking of instances and saying, "I never would have chosen THAT." It is easy to point to a spouse, boss, doctor, or life itself and say, "I did it because of them." The truth is, no one can make you do anything. Your life is of *your* making and when it comes to that great judgment day in the sky, there is no one you can point your finger at and blame. The buck stops with you. A modern shaman realizes there is no choice but to accept the consequences that come with whatever path she chooses to take. So why not choose the path you really want?

The Old and the New

In order to create the life you want, you must take responsibility for everything that is already present in your life. Until then, you will not be able to change anything. The reason this is true is because without accepting responsibility, we tend to see the cause of problems as lying *outside* ourselves, encouraging the belief that the cure will also come from *out there*. The expectation that someone else will or should fix the problem causes anger and hurt when it doesn't happen. The real causes are not resolved. It is not possible to give responsibility and the power to change over to someone or something else, and expect to be in control of your life.

Neglecting to accept the fact that you are absolutely responsible for any mess you are in blinds you to any possibility of un-creating it and sinks you into the unpleasant state of victimhood. A victim does not have the ability or power to make changes, and has lost all claim to personal authority.

Trudging along day after day, taking whatever is doled out with a sense of resignation, places the victim in a constant space of trying to survive by attempting to maintain the status quo. Once convinced that one is a servant to life and "the system," and that to change is to die, a victim may cry out that change is wanted, but will do most anything to prevent it from occurring.

Hanging on to the old while trying to bring in the new oftentimes doesn't work. Being stuck in old patterns, wounds, beliefs, habits, and programs renders us incapable of patching up a world that's just not working anymore. The only solution is to step out of it!

My friends were gone for the winter so I was taking care of their house. One day I made a quiche and put it in the oven. Since I didn't know how to use the self-cleaning feature, I put a piece of tinfoil on the bottom of the oven in case it boiled over. I set the timer and came back an hour later to take the quiche from the oven. The quiche was beautiful but the tinfoil looked like it was stuck to the oven. I tried to peel it off - it was definitely stuck. When the oven cooled I tried again to remove the foil, but it would not come off.

I wondered if running the self-cleaning feature would help, but decided to call the manufacturer for their advice. Before I even finished telling the operator the problem, she completed my sentence and told me there was probably nothing that could be done, but she would let me talk to someone else. As I began to pour out the story, the man finished it for me. He said it was a porcelain oven and the foil had fused to it much like putting a clay pot in a kiln. The only thing I could do was to replace the oven liner, which was not going to be cheap.

When strange things like this happen in my life, I figure they are trying to tell me something—kind of like a dream. After thinking about it, I realized this oven was new technology. Using tinfoil in the bottom of the oven is an old method of keeping the oven clean. I was trying to combine the old with new technology and it not only didn't work, it made a mess. The old often does not work with the new, and we have to be willing to give up the old ways to step into newer and better ways.

We Are Creators

Entertain for a moment the possibility that all the drama in life is self-created *in order to learn something.* Playing it out in real life rather than on paper or in a computer model makes the learning potential even greater. So if something is upsetting you, ask yourself why you invited a person who is hurting you to participate in your drama. What did you want that person to show you?

> *Judy and Sally were trying to work out a time to get together. Judy had a busy schedule and could not find a time to see Sally. Sally made a glib remark. Their telephone conversation ended and they hung up. The next day Judy called Sally*

and told her she had hurt her feelings with that statement and she couldn't let it go until she expressed her feelings.

Sally apologized for being insensitive and judgmental, but Judy continued to talk on about her hurt. Half an hour later the call ended with both wondering what just happened.

This raises some questions. First of all, is it possible for someone to hurt another's feelings? What happened is Judy (at some level) invited Sally to help her see some unresolved issue she was carrying. Sally (at some level) said, "I love you so much I will do that for you." She triggered Judy's old beliefs and perceived wounds, so Judy could take a closer look at them, and hopefully let them go. Of course the choice was Judy's whether she wanted to continue to blame her friend or see a greater truth about herself.

The second question that arises is, how much more empowered would Judy have felt if she had accepted responsibility for her feelings, instead of blaming her friend? What would have happened if she looked at that situation and said, "Okay, I created this; what did I want to learn?" Then she could have asked herself if there was truth in what Sally said. If there was, she could take it within and integrate the lesson, giving gratitude to Sally for helping her see it. If she found no truth then she could let it go, knowing that it was Sally's issue and nothing she had to be concerned about.

The third question is, "Do we need to continue to process stuff by beating the issue to death? Even after an apology, Judy could not let the matter rest. The reason for this was because the problem arose as a result of a wound Judy carried that had nothing to do with Sally. No matter what Sally would have said, it wouldn't change anything. It was within Judy and that is where it needed to be addressed.

Once emotional issues have been cleared, anything said to us will not have the power to affect us adversely. It is when a sensitive area gets hit that we respond. If there is no sore spot, the words go on by because they have nothing to attach to. Try this experiment: if something triggers you, accept it as an invitation from life to take a look at *why* you are affected. Discover the lesson and the person will stop doing whatever it is that upsets you, or may even disappear from your life.

A lot of energy is wasted by spending time trying to change how other people treat us. It doesn't work that way. The only way we can change another person is to correct something within ourselves—the something they are helping us learn. By looking at ourselves and seeing how we can change, we are not attempting to influence anyone else. However, the person may shift, and the way they relate to us will definitely transform, as a result of altering ourselves.

Beliefs About Power

Most people have been taught that power is a destructive force. This belief is reinforced by social structures that keep us in fear of the power and vitality we have within us. As long as we fear our power, we will not be eager to claim it. If we do not claim our power, it is up for grabs by those who want to control us.

Everyone carries fear to some degree. When this negative emotion is triggered, we feel victimized and basically say, "I am not strong enough to deal with this, so fix it for me," giving control of that area of life over to another. A good example of this is asking for more police and military protection because we don't feel safe. This is not to say we don't need it, but in the process of gaining reassurance that we are being protected, we relinquish the freedom to be out and about without being under scrutiny ourselves.

Whenever you play the victim, there will always be someone there more than willing to say, "Sure, let me handle that for you." Chances are they will give with one hand while taking with the other. As soon as you turn responsibility for yourself over to another, you have given up freedom along with your power. It can't be any other way, because freedom, power, and responsibility go hand-in-hand.

When personal power is lost, freedom soon follows. It isn't necessary to go back in history or look outside the USA to see this principle in action. We have had terrorist attacks and there are threats of more to come. The media has used these events to generate fear and bigotry in the people of this country. After the 9-11 Twin Tower attacks, people didn't want to go anywhere for fear they would be the next casualties and they screamed for protection.

The government stepped forward saying, in order to assure protection, you must submit to searches and cameras placed in all public places. E-mails, phone calls, the library books you check out, and websites you visit will be monitored. There will be a clamp down on getting post office boxes, depositing too much cash into a personal bank account, and offshore accounts definitely have to go.

People living in fear allow things like Homeland Security and the Patriot Acts. "Big Brother is watching you" is no longer a euphemism—it is reality. We are giving away our rights, while these controls have done little to stop the threats; in fact, they seem to be increasing.

Turning responsibility over to others authorizes the creation of life *by default*. This includes: wanting the government to provide health care, and in many cases, food and shelter; expecting doctors to heal our bodies; relying on policemen and the military for protection; looking to Jesus to come back and save us; asking priests and ministers to be our intermediaries to God.

This is not to say that asking for and accepting help is bad, but what are we giving up to the government, doctors, military, churches, family, and friends to get it? Consider the price of "security." It may be tempting to believe that having someone else take care of our needs will lead to good feelings, but the truth is, allowing others to make decisions for us leaves us vulnerable and without choices. There is no way to feel *good* about *that*.

False Power

Think of powerful people. Do Hitler and Saddam Hussein come to mind? It is said that they definitely had power, but this belief is based on a false idea of what power is. Having control over people and external situations is not true power. They and others like them operate through the power they *take* from other people.

Not being empowered themselves, these leaders steal power by generating fear, guilt, bigotry, anger, blame, or shame in the people and then use what they seize to control the very people they took it from. It doesn't take very many beheadings, prison sentences, or gas chamber reports before people do what they are told. These power mongers are tapping into the program most people received in childhood that says, "Follow the rules or be punished." And so they do.

Many of the people who are in control of countries, large corporations, the economic system, military, etc. know how to draw power from others, coalesce it, and put it back out as if it were their own. But if all the people stopped feeding them power for two minutes, they would crumble. It is a false power they have, but it works—for a time. Taking a peek underneath their controlling exterior reveals a powerless wounded soul, much like the Wizard of Oz.

To bring this concept closer to home, look at the playground bully. He threatens or beats up kids who are smaller because he has to make himself look important and strong. It is the same with self-serving leaders; they are really nothing more than big bullies! These power mongers are just as much victims as those they take from. If they possessed their own power, they would have no need to steal it from others.

The power they take doesn't last long so it has to be continually fed to sustain them, so their conquests have to get bigger and bigger. There is a Jim Henson movie called "The Dark Crystal". It shows how the dark beings hypnotize their subjects, take their essence and drink it, making them powerful, but the energy dwindles and they soon need another fix. It demonstrates power theft very accurately.

You may feel that this does not affect you directly and wonder what it has to do with you. As more and more controls come into play, you will find you are very much affected, unless you have learned to consciously create your world by claiming the truth of your own power. Some people are waking up to this truth and are breaking out of this confining box by changing their programming. And you can too.

Installation Of The Program

Most children live in an all-powerful world where anything is possible. They dream of flying and that money really *does* grow on trees. God—or mom, or dad, or *someone*—will take care of everything, so why worry? How long do we get to enjoy these beliefs before they are replaced with *The Program?*

- You have to work hard, and maybe with some luck, things will work out for you.
- No you can't go. We don't have the money.
- Get down or you will fall.
- Be careful or you will put your eye out.
- I don't have time.
- Do your homework and chores and if there is time, you can play. (There rarely was.)

Most of us are programmed to believe there is a lack or limited supply of good things in life, and that we have to wait until we die to reap the rewards of our suffering and servitude.

These programs and our acceptance of them take away our innocence and power. They make us feel we have no say or control in this life's experience. They cause us to believe life is a chore to get through in order to get to the good stuff that comes after death.

By teaching us the rules, our parents were not being mean; they were preparing us for the "real" world. That was their experience and they were just passing it on. Of course, the teachers, friends, and authority figures encountered along the way all helped solidify these beliefs.

The loss of power did not end in childhood. Those experiences were only preparations for more power loss in adulthood. How many people go to jobs they hate? How many people are victims of physical, emotional, mental, or verbal abuse? How many sweat bullets every spring at the thought of having to file taxes? How many put aside their dreams and talents because they fear no one will like them or that they will be thought of as weird? How many people do not speak their true feelings or beliefs for fear of repercussions?

Following *The Program* assures the giving away of power every day of our lives. Many people are so accustomed to living in a controlled environment, they don't even realize it is happening and if they do, don't know how to prevent it.

The truth is, *The Program* has a TERMINATE button. We *can* stop the cycle!

True Power

Power has gotten a bad rap because of the widely held belief that power corrupts. Power does not corrupt and it is not bad. When we are in possession of our power, it is not a destructive force. It is energy we can use to create what we want. Being responsible for ourselves and living as empowered beings can only bring balance and harmony into our lives. NOT being empowered is the cause of destruction, chaos, and pain, because that state is what produces the temptation or mandate to *take power away from someone else.*

In order to claim our power we have to understand what it is. True power is an energy that comes from within us. It is the ability to direct our own lives. It is making our own choices. It is standing in our truth so that the bullies of the world do not choose us as their next easy mark or victim. It is the freedom to express self, which, if we were taught correctly from the time we were children, means we are free to express as long as our freedom doesn't limit or restrict someone else. It is having respect for others and ourselves. It is taking responsibility for our lives and what happens to us.

Sometimes it is not easy to be in your power because it means you can no longer be a "sheeple"—people following like sheep. When you are in your power, you do your own thinking, and make your own decisions. You may seek advice from others, but ultimately you make the choices, taking full responsibility for them. Your thoughts and actions

may not always be popular, but people respect you—
sometimes unconsciously—for speaking, acting and being
in your truth, even if they don't understand or agree with
you. And if they *don't* respect you for being yourself, you
might not want them in your life anyway.

So how is lost power regained? Start by taking responsibility for everything that is in your life. You may look at
your life and say, "There is no way I created this mess."
Instead be brave and say, "It is time to stop the blame game
and get truthful with myself. I created this, and I can un-
create it."

> *True power comes in direct proportion*
> *to the amount of responsibility we are*
> *willing to accept for ourselves.*
> *That is the key.*

Life supports us in getting what we want. With clarity,
the desired results can come quite quickly.

A friend wanted some sage from an
area she was visiting, but did not have
time before she left to go out and shop for
it. She had no sooner told this to the per-
son she was visiting, when the doorbell
rang. It was someone selling sage bun-
dles.

Once we are clear about what we want, we can have it, as long as it is in accord with our highest good and is not interfering with another person's rights.

Years ago I cut an advertisement from the paper. It said:

"GET REAL, AUTHENTIC, GENUINE,
BONA-FIDE, LEGITIMATE, GUARANTEED,
HONEST-TO-GOODNESS."

To be anything less is to lose power.

So get real. Claim responsibility for what happens to you, both good and bad. We have been talking about the less than perfect times, but be sure to also acknowledge yourself when good comes your way. Doing so confirms that you are on the right track in creating the life you want.

Time To Remember

You will live as a controlled person until you decide it no longer works for you. You may have been comfortable in this scenario at one time, but if you truly want to move towards wholeness, it will no longer work. You must awaken to the power within you and claim your sovereignty. Life as we know it is changing. We can either change with it or succumb.

In order to live freely, it is necessary to accept responsibility for your life just as it is, but it is important to make a conscious choice in the matter. Life without freedom consists of bondage, pain and victimhood. Alternately, you may choose to live the life of a modern shaman: joyful, free, and sovereign.

Exercise: Getting an Overview

It will be helpful to get an overview of life to know exactly where you are at this time. So take an inventory. You can write this out or just give it some thought—whatever works best for you.

Take the different areas of life, i.e. work, relationships, income, health, spirituality, family, etc. and examine what you like and dislike about each. Do you feel good about it or would you like things to be different?

As you do this, see yourself as the creator of your life, and as such, know you have the power to change anything that no longer works for you. What would you change? How would you change it? Let your writing take you into areas you haven't explored before.

Once you determine what you want to change, it is important to get clear about what you want instead. You probably know what you don't want—you have had plenty of experience with that—but you may not have a clear picture of what you *do* want.

Remember, you have been operating under *The Program*, "Follow the rules or be punished," which did not leave room for getting in touch with your feelings and inner desires. You are wiser now, and it is time to discover what really motivates you and move toward it.

You needn't do anything with this writing; it is just an inventory of your life and an assessment of your thoughts and feelings about it. It is finding your starting point, so you can chart your course as you work through the exercises in this book.

Chapter 3
Etheric Clearing

If you realized how powerful your thoughts are, you would never think a negative thought.

Unknown

Creation Tools

Once you realize you have created the lesser desired aspects of your life, you can look at how you did it in order to find ways to *undo* it. The basic life-creating process is accomplished through thought and emotion. This is not some new age concept; it is a scientific fact. Thinking a thought releases a chemical in the brain. That chemical stimulates an emotion within us. The emotion causes us to think more similar thoughts, which produce more chemical reactions. It sets a cycle in motion. To make changes, we have to break that cycle.

If you don't like what is happening to you, the answer is to change your thoughts. The process of creation is the same, but you consciously change your thoughts to ones that support what you want, instead of what you don't want. These thoughts release chemicals that allow emotions to arise that create more positive thoughts. This releases more harmonious chemicals that produce more good emotions. This is how we get off the merry-go-round of dissatisfying creations. It takes some discipline to get this process started, but once set in motion, it builds upon itself and gets easier. You may want to do some research on using positive affirmations, as they would be most helpful in this process.

The thing that keeps most people from thinking progressive thoughts is their history. People are victims to their wounds and slaves to their beliefs, attitudes, judgments, and programming. This patterning is old and must be released in order to move into conscious living.

All In The Interpretation

It is easy to get entangled in emotional pain and to wear it like a badge of honor. Identifying with such a state and expecting others to honor us for all we have been through prevents the realization that *emotional wounding is an illusion!* There is nothing wrong with us and we don't need to heal anything. It is true that some of life's experiences are traumatic. Going through such experiences can leave you feeling that you have no control over the circumstances affecting you. This can cause you to move into fear and resistance and to subsequently feel pain.

The pain is not from the event itself; it is caused by fear and resistance *in response* to the event. Fear and resistance block the flow of energy, which then collects in the weakest part of self. That clot of blocked energy is the true source of pain.

If the event were the real cause of pain, all people would feel the same from the same event, but this is not the case. While everyone goes into fear and resistance at some point in life, it is our individual responses to past experience that produce our unique triggers.

For example, one person loses a job and feels suicidal. Another person has the same experience but looks at it as an opportunity to do something she always wanted to do. In this case, the removal of a job that *seemed* necessary for security is, in fact, a liberation! Because that job security is no longer there, she is free to explore other options.

Another example is when someone dies. Loss, regret, and loneliness are not the only possible responses. Not everyone feels the same way. Some find happiness from receiving an inheritance. Others celebrate that the person has moved on to a better place. Someone else is relieved that a long and trying episode of care-taking has come to an end.

It is different for each of us because our past experiences are not the same. When something happens, we interpret it based on past experience and information. If we don't have anything just like it, we find something in our memory banks that is similar to it. A tough experience in childhood may form the basis for our response to challenges in adulthood. If we felt safe, loved and protected by our parents, we react to the present situation as if that were true today. If, instead, we felt threatened, abandoned, and left to get through it as best we could, we may react the same as that scared little child from our past.

Our feelings toward what happens to us today are largely based on past events and what emotions we stored with those memories. I have a friend who was raped by three men. When it happened, she let their energy shoot up her spine and out the top of her head—she did not hold onto the force and hatred of women they projected into her. She had no control over what was happening to her body, but she did have control over how she handled it. She chose not to interpret the event as something horrible that happened to her, but something that empowered her. She saw that no matter how bad things can be she could remain in her place of empowerment.

There are many children who are raised in abusive families. When they grow up, some will tell you it ruined their lives. Others will say that those experiences made them better parents, got them great jobs, or helped them have more compassion for others. Our thoughts and feelings determine how we interpret what happens in our lives. Do we see the event as a wound or an opportunity? The choice is ours.

Our wounds are illusions, but we also need to deal with the reality we are presently experiencing or we go further into denial. If you feel you have been wounded and require healing, you need to honor that as your starting place. We deal with the illusion as if it was real, but it isn't wise to get stuck there. People sometimes spend years in psychotherapy when it may not be necessary at all.

It is impossible to heal the past because there is nothing wrong with it. There is nothing wrong with us. It is all in how we have interpreted the experiences we have had. These are just rough spots in the road of life and it would be beneficial to accept a new perspective about such experiences. Then we can go forward with a new gauge for what we encounter. Remember, how you choose to interpret your experiences from here on out will determine whether you develop more wounds or create opportunities.

The Backpack

Since there are events that cause us to feel over-whelmed, we have developed a handy little device that I call the backpack. When we encounter a situation we don't feel equipped to handle at that moment, we treat it as an "I'll-look-at-it-later" item. True, we have to deal with it at some point, but just not right now. Once something is pitched over the shoulder into the bag, we tend to forget about it.

Since people seldom live in the present, we use our baggage for survival. If we had to make every decision every day without anything to guide us, we would never get anywhere. We'd be spending all of our time trying to de-termine a course of action. So we have this storehouse of ready-made decisions, attitudes, judgments, tradition, and beliefs to help us make choices. Since we created this stor-age place early in life, it has a lot of information but much of it is outdated for today's living. Despite that, we continue to use the contents until we figure out there has to be a bet-ter way. That is when we begin making changes.

The items in your bag don't magically go away, and time does not heal all wounds. The backpack allows you to set things aside until another day, when you may be stronger and better able to deal with them. During the times you feel strong and ready, you can reach over your shoulder and draw something out of the pack. You can consider it, gain understanding of where it came from, why it's there, and how you can use it to your benefit; or, you can just get rid of it.

People use their backpacks when they can't—or choose not to—deal with something. If it isn't cleaned out periodically, it gets heavier and heavier, as the process of living collects more and more baggage. Up to a certain point, carrying the bag causes us to develop strength; but eventually it becomes too heavy to drag around. Then there is a choice to make. We can become conscious, choosing to take obsolete stuff out of the bag, or remain unconscious until the body tires of the load, producing an inevitable experience of disease.

Refusal to look at something in the bag denies that experience. This lessens the pain, but also blocks the benefits. The answer is to give the experience full attention in that moment and by doing this become able to release it. When the backpack is empty, we no longer need it. Old programs will be gone, having no place to be stored. Our responses become light and free, determined by our consciousness in the moment.

Etheric Clearing

It is okay to take your time emptying your backpack. It doesn't have to be done all at once and there is no need to re-experience past traumas. By removing an experience from the bag, recognizing it, finding the lesson associated with it, and integrating it, we are empowered to let the experience go. This is an alchemical process called etheric clearing. It is *etheric* because parts of ourselves not normally seen with our physical eyes are being addressed. As we discover the goodies that are in the backpack along with the stuff we chose to ignore, we become inspired to dig deeper and empty even more of its contents. It is then that we begin to enjoy the benefits of the experiences we have had.

Etheric clearing is based on a quantum physics principle that says parts of an atom respond according to the thoughts and feelings of the observer. Since all life on this planet is made up of atoms, we construct our life and our body by the intentions we hold. If we intend to have health and well being, we move towards them in our thoughts and feelings and the outcome is a true state of health. While it is possible for this to happen instantly, for many people it may take time to reach a totally healthy state. It will take as long as it takes, but with each item cleared we feel lighter and more whole. The length of time becomes unimportant.

If the thought arises that you could never do this work for yourself, consider that this is *your* body and *your* life we are talking about. Who could possibly know your body better than you? *You* know what hurts, and if you stop and think about it, you also know where the blockages are. You just need to know what to look for and gain a few tools to help you clear them. There may be times you need assistance, but much can be done on your own. Doing so helps you realize the self-empowered being you truly are.

Caring for yourself is not as hard as some might like you to believe. You just need to be willing to claim the responsibility for the way things are in your life and take steps to change what you don't like. The changes need not be huge, as even the little ones can shift things in big ways. It is like a kaleidoscope. Turn it the tiniest bit and the whole image shifts. If you change one thing in your life, it can have dramatic results. Begin with the premise that you *have* the power *and* responsibility for your world.

Sometimes the first thing to clear is any doubt about whether or not you can do this work for yourself. The solution is to *try it*. You'll never know until you do. Prove it to yourself. By understanding the information in this book and following the exercises laid out, you just may surprise yourself. You may or may not have stupendous results at first, but if you keep at it, you will become more aware of the energy flowing inside you and the results you are creating.

The following is one person's perspective on doing an etheric clearing.

> *To speak of etheric clearing is a pleasure. Though I have done much work, I found this work to be exceptional. I have removed energies and blockages that were holding me back in my growth. The work is unique to me and it has given me a wholeness I have never known. It changed me and allowed me to reach new heights in my personal and spiritual growth. After doing the work, I have felt so elated. The work is in the energy field, not the physical body, yet it is powerful and life changing.*

Intention

Intention is the most powerful tool at your disposal for manifesting what you want, because it combines thought and feeling to determine the outcome of everything you do. Not all of your intentions are consciously chosen. Sometimes you may think thoughts and have feelings that you are not even aware of having. These thoughts and feelings influence your life as much as those you consciously choose, because *all* of them are energized when attention is placed on them, whether consciously chosen or not.

Thoughts and feelings work in tandem to create your world, but what happens when they are in conflict with each other? If in your mind you ask for something but don't really feel you can have it, or if you actually feel a greater need in another area, you may not receive what you asked for. Here is an example. Suppose you experience a health challenge and set the intent to get well. At the same time what you *really* want is spiritual growth. Perhaps the purpose of your health issue is to help you take strides forward in your spiritual awareness. In this case, you may not come into better health until you gain the wisdom you were seeking on a spiritual level from that experience.

It is important, when asking for something, that you feel life's abundance, for this allows you to keep your energy field open to receive. If a request is made from a place of fear or doubt, the energy shuts down or becomes distorted. What comes back may not be what you wanted. In fact, it could actually be the opposite.

You needn't be concerned with HOW something will manifest. That is up to Spirit. Allow the results to come in whatever way is best for you. When your answer comes back, it could appear as if your request was denied. It is then your challenge to either trust that it was exactly what you needed in that moment or to restate your intent more clearly.

If another person is setting an intention for you, it is important that they be coming from a place of respect and integrity. Etheric clearing is one area where this is especially true because of your openness during the process. It could cause many challenges if the person petitions for something that is not in alignment with your best and highest good, or if they use your openness to their own advantage.

> *Ginny studied with a psychic teacher for a year. She came to me after she left his group because she suspected he had taken control of her life. We found that he had embedded numerous energies in her*

and was draining her power. This teacher was able to gain the initial control by hav-ing people attend free meditations and healings he offered at his metaphysical school.

Ginny had put him above herself be-lieving he had her answers, so when she opened to receive energy from him, she gave her power to him and allowed him to implant her. Through these implanted en-ergies, he was able to take her power and keep her coming back. This happened be-cause she believed she was powerless and needed his guidance.

Intention can be used or abused. Once you observe how you are using intention in your life, you can stop at-tracting things you don't want and manifest those you do. You can accomplish anything by setting your intent and moving toward it by what you think and feel.

The Senses

In doing etheric clearing, it helps to be in tune with the inner self. This is not difficult once you develop a method of communication. This will be unique for each of you, and it is important to avoid setting your expectations by what works for others. This usually leads to frustration and disregarding the information that you do receive.

In the physical body, we have five senses – touch, taste, smell, hearing, and sight. We use these to gather information. Each of our etheric bodies (supra-physical, emotional, mental, memory, unconscious, and spiritual bodies— we will discuss these later) also have these senses. This is how they communicate with us. We get a feeling. We hear a voice. We have a vision. We get a bad taste in our mouth. We smell something. That is our inner self sending us a message.

Sometimes one sense is stronger than the others. This is true of our inner senses as well as our outer ones. Hearing can be strong while visual acuity is weak. Knowing how your outer senses work in relation to each other will help, because your inner senses work the same way. If you are kinesthetic, you predominately gather information through feeling. Find your strongest sense and begin working with that one. Chances are, whatever sense is strongest in the physical will also be the strongest in the inner. Once you get used to using that sense, the others may open so that you can access them all.

Reasons for Clearing

The reasons for doing a clearing are numerous, but the following are examples of when you might choose this route to resolution. If you are feeling agitated, blocked, confused, stuck, or have experienced a health challenge, car accident, near death experience, surgery, death of a loved one, or hard times, you may want to consider doing some clearing work. Basically anytime you are not feeling balanced and in harmony with the world or yourself, you could do some etheric clearing.

Etheric clearing can be done as often as you feel the need. After most sessions, the work is integrated and becomes part of your reality immediately, but if a major paradigm shift occurs, it could take longer. The average integration period is 24 hours. No one can tell you the timing that is right for you. It takes as long as it takes.

Once the work is integrated, you may be ready to do more work immediately, or you may not be ready for another session for six months. It is important to pay attention to your body, allowing it to tell you what it needs. In this way you claim your power by deciding what is right for you.

Limitations

Etheric clearings work according to intention, and there is no limit to what can be accomplished with intent. The results of a clearing are totally open. The only limitations are those placed by you. The following are some ways you may block your progress with the clearing work.

When you first start working with the etheric energies, fear and skepticism may be present. It is normal to have some concerns when approaching something unfamiliar. You also may be hesitant for fear you will find out some-thing "bad" about yourself, or worse yet, that another will, and you will be judged as a bad person.

People have been taught to harshly judge everything, especially their own selves. When you think you are unwor-thy of feeling good, you block the process. No good can come to you when you feel you deserve to be punished. The truth is, there is nothing "bad" about you. You are a beauti-ful and wondrous being. Unfortunately, because of pro-gramming, you may not always see that.

Excessive use of drugs and alcohol can slow the bene-fits of the clearing work if the user does not want to make changes. However if one is in the process of healing this dependency, the clearings can be of great benefit.

Etheric clearing is just the beginning. Once we begin emptying our backpack and release the illusion of separation, woundedness, and pain, we can enter into a state of wholeness. This need not take a long time or be a slow, laborious process. We can do it swiftly and step with ease and grace into a naturally empowered state that is a modern shaman's birthright.

Exercise: Emptying Your Backpack

Understanding a situation makes it easier to clear. It is helpful to *write* to get information. Writing is a wonderful tool for empowerment. You can use it to gain understanding, to release pent up emotions, to step back and look at the bigger picture, to keep track of thoughts and ideas, and anything else your creative mind can think up.

Not all people enjoy writing, but try it and see how it works for you. For those of you who want or need it, I have included this writing exercise. You can do it before doing any clearing work in order to get clarity about the deeper issue. It gives you a place to begin.

When you take something from your pack, you need a way of identifying it. You can use the following exercise to do this.

Jot down the important events of your day. It would be difficult to include everything that you experienced so write the thoughts or events that stand out for you. These things come forward because there is something connected with them that is of interest to you. It may be something another person would not even notice, but to you, it is like a neon light. It could be as minor as a line in a song like, "She believes in me." It stands out for a reason.

Once you have the major events listed, take one and use the statement you wrote about it. Explore that image and just start writing. What was your part in it? Why was it important to you? How did you feel? What did you learn? Let the writing take you anywhere it will. Accept whatever comes; don't worry whether your writing style is proper or the words are precise, if it is manly or ladylike. Just write. No one is going to read it but you.

If you only have a few minutes to review your day, examine only one event. It is possible that most experiences revolve around a central theme so examining more than one would only help to clarify the issue or confirm that resolution is needed in that area.

As you explore your thoughts and feelings about the events of your day, you dig into old patterns, conditioning and training, which may have lain dormant for many years.

These unaccepted parts want to be recognized and if you don't welcome them to the surface, they may erupt at inopportune times.

Sometimes the experience you examine is a happy, wonderful event. It is beneficial to look at these times as well as the painful ones when writing, because you can learn much by being aware of what it feels like to experience pleasure or success. It is good to also see how you brought the good things into your life so you can create similar events.

Now that you are aware of your backpack, you can check each day to see what new things you have stored there, oftentimes without even knowing it. You decide as you sort through the items in the bag whether today is the day to examine them. Perhaps they need immediate attention or maybe they are best left stashed until some later date. It's your bag, and it's your choice.

Chapter 4
Setting the Stage

You are an extension of Source Energy. You are standing on the Leading Edge of thought. Your time-space reality was set into motion through the power of thought long before it manifested in the physical form in which you see it now.

Esther and Jerry Hicks
Ask And It Is Given

Curtain Up

With any good performance the stage must be set before the curtain goes up and the performers enter. The audience would be confused if the wrong setting was on stage or if the stagehands began bringing items on after the scene had begun.

The same is true when doing an etheric clearing. Setting the stage is done on a physical, as well as subtle level. By setting the space in which to work, we open to greater awareness, bring in the clearing energies, protect ourselves, and keep the area free of energies as they are released. Creating the space is not difficult to do. Like the rest of the work, it is done with intent.

Getting Grounded

Getting stabilized and connected to the earth energy should be a way of life, but definitely something done before starting any energy work. This is called being grounded. Grounding is something many "spiritual" people do not want to do and for some people it is not easy. It was not something that came easily for me either.

Most of my life I spent half in and half out of my body. I didn't particularly want to be in a physical body because life felt heavy, so I did not commit to being fully present. I knew I wasn't grounded and didn't see any need to be. I even found a religion that taught out-of-body travel and I followed it for twenty years. It's not as if I needed instruction doing this, but I liked it because it reinforced that which was comfortable to me.

One summer I was given the opportunity to live on a ranch in South Dakota. Some friends had an awesome little two-bedroom house on their property that was vacant and they wanted someone to live in it. The house had been home to a couple and their children. Even though the family had not lived there for some time, I could still feel the family energy. It felt really good.

I drove 100 miles into town once a week and saw my neighbors periodically. Most of my days passed without seeing or talking to other humans. I never felt lonely because many spirit beings came to be with me. They kept me company, taught me, and protected me.

I spent my days making paper, writing, doing art projects, and tending my garden. I had not had a garden in many years, so I asked the fairies and other nature spirits to help me. At first they were hesitant, but once they realized I honored the earth and truly wanted to work with them, they instructed me in the care of the soil and the plants. Their lessons were always to the point and given with love. It was a gentle, nurturing time for me.

When I planted the garden, I put out some broccoli plants and the next morning there were only sticks left standing. It was time to talk to the rabbits. I told them if they ate the plants when they were so young, there would be no garden. I said if they left them alone until they were bigger, there would be enough food for all of us. They never bothered any of the young plants again.

The spring rains had been plentiful so the cherry tree was loaded with fruit. I picked all I wanted and asked my neighbor if she wanted some. She said she had enough to do putting up the raspberries from her garden. I went to the tree and thanked it for all the wonderful fruit it had provided for me.

The next day my neighbor called and said she changed her mind and would like some cherries, so I went out to the tree to pick some for her. There was not a single cherry left on the tree—overnight it had been stripped clean!

Just 24 hours before, the tree was full of fruit—where had it all gone? I asked the nature spirits and they told me that the birds and animals had waited until I had what I wanted, and once I was finished, they came and ate from the tree. They had honored the agreement I had made with the rabbits. I have never felt such gratitude and humbleness.

Being in the presence of these joyous, loving beings was a gift for me. City life had closed my eyes, ears, and heart to nature. These beings lovingly taught me to work with the unseen world and showed me that being connected to the earth we were born from brought with it a feeling of well-being, not pain. They also taught me a new respect for all life. I felt at one with all beings, visible and invisible.

During this time, my diet consisted of organic fruits and vegetables fresh from the earth. My days were spent outdoors in clean air. Walking barefoot in the dirt, digging in the soil, and watching the plants grow, I felt alive. I awoke every day to the songs of birds and fell asleep to the sounds of crickets, frogs, and the howl of coyotes. I felt healthy, happy, fulfilled, and safe for the first time in my life. I was grounded and it felt soooooo good.

That summer on the ranch showed me that being grounded did not mean heaviness and that the human experience is not about suffering. There is happiness, aliveness, wholeness, connection, and beauty to be enjoyed. When we are living these things, we are open and free. It does not hold us back spiritually either, because when we feel safe and joyous, we are able to expand into greater inner experiences.

My life on the ranch helped me connect to my body and to the earth. In order to live fully, we each have to find our own way to do this. Not all people would like living that close to the earth.

We can have some success in the clearing work without being totally grounded, but it is much easier and safer the more connected we are.

Staying Neutral

In order to be successful with self-clearing, you must remain neutral before, during, and after the clearing. If there is judgment of self, the problem, the energies you are clearing, or the outcome, there will be obstructions in the energy flow. This can inhibit the work, because, if you are stuck in judgment, you won't be able to see the whole picture.

It can be difficult to stay neutral. People are taught to have an opinion about everything and everyone, but if this work is to be accomplished in integrity, it is necessary to remain free of judgment. The best way is to stay grounded and in the light.

If you are helping another do this work, it is doubly important to stay out of judgment. When in judgment, there is a tendency to project your reality onto the other person and it opens you to "taking on" that person's stuff. Then you have to clear it from *your* life.

Trust

Imagination is the language of the soul. We have been taught that imagination is just whimsy and not to be trusted. Logic is what we are told to base our thoughts and actions upon.

In doing the clearing work, you may see something in your mind's eye or feel something and it often appears as if there is no logic in what is presented. If you remain open to what is being shown, the logic will follow. Many times you may see or hear something and have no clue what it means, but if you stay with it, it will all become clear and make perfect sense. You may just need more information before the whole picture can be seen. Only by trusting and accepting what is shown can you learn what needs to be done to clear the situation.

If you don't take things as they are given, you miss the steppingstones laid out for you and are unable to move on. If you are grounded and have set the space well, you need have no fear that anything but truth will present itself.

Sensing Energy

As you work with energy, you may or may not *feel* it. Sometimes people expect it to feel a certain way and when it doesn't, they think nothing is happening. If it doesn't feel like you think it "should" feel, just keep going. The validation will come in the changes that result in your life.

There are many different ways of feeling energy. You may get truth chills or goose bumps. It is confirmation that you are on the right track. You may feel a pulsating in the palms of your hands. This is the energy flowing through them. You may experience a wave of warmth in your body, as the energy flows through it.

The first time I did a clearing, my hands got all prickly. It felt as if my hands were cold and I had put them in hot water—not a pleasant sensation, but it did let me know something was happening. This went away as soon as I stopped the session and eventually I got used to the additional flow of energy when I worked, so it no longer happened. If you have trouble feeling energy, you may want to take a Reiki class where the instructor will help you become aware of the energy flow.

It is not necessary to feel the energy in order for it to work, but it is a confirmation that you are accomplishing something. Human nature likes validation. You may also find that when you are working on yourself, it is not as easy to sense energy as it is when you are working on another person. This is often the case. It makes sense because when you touch your own arm, you don't have the same sensation as when someone else touches it.

Helpers and Guides

Clearings are rarely performed solo, so the first thing to consider is finding inner helper beings—your support crew.

This work is done at an energetic level and you will benefit greatly by having at least one being that you can trust to do whatever is needed for your best and highest good. Perhaps you already are aware of your guides and helpers, but there may be new ones that come in while you are doing this work.

If you are not aware of any beings working with you, ask to be assigned those helpers who will be the best support crew for you. All you have to do is intend that this be so. Always put in the stipulation that they and everything you do with the etheric clearing work be done for your best and highest good and the highest good of all.

Once you have asked for and are connected with your helpers, dialogue with them to get to know and trust them. It might be helpful to write down a question for them, listen for the answer, and then jot that down. Listening to them in these dialogue sessions will help train your inner ears so you can better hear them during the clearing work. This will be one of the primary ways they will give you information on what steps to take to clear an issue.

When calling in your helpers, it is well to stop a moment and see, feel, or listen to them. After some practice, you come to recognize their energy. This will keep you from being fooled if other beings come in and want to work with you. If at any time the energy that comes in does not feel like love and light, challenge it. The beings that come to work with you will never get angry or lose patience. If they do, they are not the highest energy you can be working with and you would do well to tell them to leave.

One of the most effective group of beings I have worked with is a group I call the spiritual surgeons. They are light beings that help with the etheric clearing work. They are very willing to be of assistance, but will wait to be asked to help because they will not enter your space without an invitation.

They work on the bodies and chakras with speed, precision, dexterity, and grace. They are very effective at doing their job. They can provide anything needed for your clearing. They often take you to an etheric place called the energy chambers where they work with light and sound and any other technologies they feel are needed. They work quickly, painlessly, and effectively. They are truly masters when it comes to the clearing arts.

The surgeons often appear as tall, thin, white, wispy light beings. One lady who saw these beings asked about her lower back pain. Then she saw herself on a table. She could see her spine but they had not opened up the skin. The spine had an attachment that twisted around it, making her very uncomfortable. This had been there since she was eight years old. Since it was not in her highest and best good for it to remain, the surgeons removed it for her.

The helpers appear differently to different people. One lady who works with the fairy kingdom saw her helpers as golden gnomes. She was learning to channel beings and they smoothed away the blockages in her throat. They also worked on her ears using various sounds. Another lady saw her helpers as little light bulbs that twirled around. They put little hoses inside her body and flushed it out with liquid light. This was an image she could use to understand what they were doing. So if your helpers seem to work in an unconventional manner, it may be because they are using metaphors you can understand.

Sometimes your helper beings come in for a particular job and then you may not see them in your clearing sessions again for a long time. They could be guides or counselors who came in to give you a new perspective or information on something that is troubling you. Jesus and Mary may come to work on your heart. Power animals often appear in order to gather up pieces. Your inner self knows what is needed and your intent is the tool it uses to call in the help you need. That help can come in many different forms.

When setting the space to work in, there are many re-
sources available to us. Our guides want us to clear out the
old and grow as much as we are ready to grow. You will
never be alone in doing this work—help is always there for
you to draw on; all you have to do is ask. This is something
you can absolutely trust.

In working with the helpers, guidance will come from
them as well as from your divine self. In the big picture
there is no difference, as we are all one. Sometimes it is just
easier to listen, if you think you are talking to someone
other than your higher self. You will become familiar with
the feeling of each being you work with and recognize who
is with you at any given time. It just takes practice.

Power Animals

Sometimes it is hard to connect with guides or to accept that they want to work with you. If this is the case, it
may be easier to work with a power animal. Since there are
animals that you can see, touch, and hear in this physical
reality, they may feel more real to you.

Working with a power animal can be of great assistance. To find your animal totem, close your eyes and ask
to be shown. By observing and accepting the first image
that comes into your inner view screen, you will know what

your power animal is. If you are shown an animal, you may tend to disregard it because the animal is one you would never suspect, like the porcupine. It does not seem like a powerful animal but the spirit of every animal carries what the Native Americans call "medicine." Each animal has a different medicine (or gift) to offer. For more information, read *Animal Speak,* by Ted Andrews, to learn about animals and the gifts they have to share.

Your animal totem shares its medicine and you can call on it to give you energy and strength. You can rely on its power to come to your aid at any time. Maybe your totem has been with you since childhood. Perhaps as a youngster, a certain animal fascinated you. If so, this may be your power animal.

A totem may come to work with you for a short time or be a lifelong companion. There may be several animals you work with, each for a different purpose. This is an individual matter and can be different for everyone. As you build a relationship with your totem, you will come to trust that this energy is present and working with you.

The Script

Before beginning any work, be it teaching a class, doing a session, earth energy work, etc., I set the space in which to work. One time I forgot.

> *I was presenting a paper I had written. I walked onto the stage to give my presentation and nothing seemed to be flowing. I was having a hard time focusing and my tongue was tripping over the words. A big, planted tree on the stage tipped over and no one was anywhere near it. Something was trying to get my attention. I paused and realized I had forgotten to set the energies, so I stopped and did it right then and the rest of the talk went very well.*

Your intention is much more important than exactly what you do to set the space. The one thing you want to be sure to *intend* is that the work be for the best and highest good for all concerned. You can word this in whatever way feels right, but it is important to do it every time you work. Make this a habit.

When giving a talk, you don't have to be standing on stage when you say the script. Do it before going on. The important thing is to do it, because the energy may not flow where you want it to if the space is not first created for it. It is like pouring water without a vessel to catch it—it goes wherever gravity takes it. So get yourself ready to receive the energy that is to come through, by repeating the following statement or something similar.

> I set up a vortex of light and sound for protection and to carry away or transmute anything that is no longer serving my highest good, and to bring in truth and clarity. I invite in my teachers, guides, the spiritual surgeons, angelic forces, power animals, my divine self—that part that connects to the Divine Source God—and anyone who is willing to work with me for my highest good and the highest good of all.

In repeating your script, you have called in guidance so all is done in the highest manner. You have set up a way to dispose of anything that could be harmful to others or be reabsorbed by you. You have brought in your helpers and asked for protection, invoking an intention to perceive in a higher way. Until this is done, you do not have a protected space in which to work. This leaves you open to any forces that may want to interfere with the work.

To be protected and working in the highest energy, it is necessary to have these components in place before you begin, especially if you are helping another do this work. If this is overlooked or done haphazardly, you can open yourself to taking on the responsibility, issues, and energies the other person releases.

Many practitioners have given up working on certain clients because they could not handle the repercussions. They blamed the clients for what happened when it was really their own misunderstanding of how to work with energies that caused the problem.

Exercise:
Working with Spiritual Surgeons

It is best to find a time and place where you are comfortable and will not be disturbed for about 30 minutes. That means also turning the phone off. It is okay to lie down or sit in a chair, whatever works for you. Lighting candles may be of help, but it could also keep your mind occupied, wondering if the wax is running on the furniture. Applying or diffusing essential oils may help. Music can help set the mood, but it could also interfere by taking you in another direction—you may find yourself following the music rather than sticking with the work. So try different things and see what works for you. The main thing is to be comfortable, so you can relax.

If you relax too much you may find yourself falling asleep. However, sometimes this is just what is needed because the mind may need to be out of the way to get the work done. You will know if this is the case by the results you experience. If nothing is changing in your life and you keep falling asleep, the written exercises might work better for you, as they will help you stay more alert. Again, experiment to see what works.

It is necessary to create a safe space in the inner as well as in the physical environment. To create the inner environment, use your intention. Put yourself in a swirling, cone-shaped vortex of light and sound for protection. This light and sound energy comes down the center of the vortex in a clockwise direction. The negative energies you are releasing are carried up the outside of the funnel in a counterclockwise direction.

It will look like a spiral of light and you may hear a sound connected with it. This light illuminates areas for clearer vision. The light and sound transmute old patterns and break up stuck energies. They also carry away the debris that is released.

When you repeat your script to call in etheric beings to work with you, it is important to stipulate that they only come to work for your best and highest good and the good of all. You do not want to leave yourself open to any beings that are not of the light. Remember each step is done by your intent—you don't have to MAKE anything happen.

> Call in the light, your guides, power animals, the angelic forces, and your divine self by saying the script given above, or the one you have created for yourself. Your helpers will assist or just watch over you as the spiritual surgeons work. Set the intent of what you want to happen.

> Through intent, open your energy field for your helpers to work. As they proceed, you may hear or intuit what happened to cause this condition in your body or your life. You may get some understanding about the issue or information regarding what you need to change in order to clear it. You need not do anything but remain open.

> You want to restore the body to health, but more importantly you want to

clear the issue that created the physical condition. If you do not take care of the cause, the problem will return, perhaps manifested in another form. You do not need to be aware of everything, however, as sometimes it is old stuff and you just need to let it go.

As your helpers work, you might feel a sensation in some part of your body. Don't try to force anything, just let it happen. You can watch, feel and listen as the surgeons work. When they finish, thank everyone who worked with you.

If you do not have time for this exercise during your awake time, you can request that the surgeons come during dreamtime. Just intend when you go to sleep that you go into the light with the surgeons and that they do the work you need. You may sleep soundly or you may have a difficult time sleeping. If this happens, just ask them to regulate the energy so you can sleep while they work. You may or may not have recall of the work that was done.

Using Complementary Modalities

Once you get settled and have said your script, you can "turn on" the Reiki, if you are attuned to it. You can use essential oils, Touch for Health, or any other modalities with which you are familiar. They complement this work very well, as they help the flow of energy through the bodies. By incorporating other modalities into this work, you will be expressing yourself in your own unique way. If you do not work with other modalities, don't worry that things won't work for you, they will. All you need to do is intend that the highest energy flow through you.

Chapter 5
The Seven Bodies

The mind is its own place, and in itself can
make a Heav'n of Hell or a Hell of Heav'n.

John Milton

By Definition

Many authors have given various definitions of the bodies. It is important that we all begin on the same page in doing this work, so I want to explain how I see them. The view I am presenting here is perhaps over-simplified, but it is the easiest way I have found to explain how they work both individually and as a total package.

A human being is whole—complete in every way—but sometimes it is easier to understand something by looking at its parts. There are seven bodies through which we gain experience: physical, supra-physical, emotional, memory, mental, unconscious, and spiritual. The bodies are not stacked like pancakes, as you may have seen in books. Such illustrations are simply a representation for our linear minds. The bodies are more like layers around the physical body that encircle us in a 360-degree fashion. There is some delineation between them, but they also blend and weave together.

As you go through your day, you are very busy experiencing and recording everything that happens. There is no getting away from it. Everything that is stored will be the seed cause for future experiences. Knowing that your past does not just go away because you forget about it is good motivation for doing the etheric clearing because you then have less baggage to drag around.

The bodies all have their own chakra and sensory systems, yet none operates independently—they are all connected. What happens in one, affects us on all levels. That is why it is important to have the bodies all working together. When they are, we know our direction, we feel in harmony with ourselves, and life flows much easier.

The Physical Body

The physical body can be likened to a hard copy of our subtle bodies. Whatever programs or data exist in the subtle bodies will manifest at some point into the physical. This could take years, months, days, or minutes. If given enough time, it will happen. Whether these thoughts and emotions are happy or unhappy doesn't matter—it works the same.

The physical body is the one with which we are all familiar. You can look in a mirror and see it. You can touch it and feel it. It takes in information through the five senses - tasting, hearing, touching, seeing, and smelling. This all seems pretty straight forward, but is it that simple? Let's take a closer look.

This physical body is our vehicle for experiencing the three-dimensional reality, but discerning what sense we are using is sometimes confusing. For instance when you listen to music, the eardrums vibrate and you are able to hear the music. At the same time, though you may not be aware of it, your whole body is vibrating with the frequency of each beat. This is how deaf people can also experience music. Have you ever wondered how Beethoven composed timeless music despite the fact that he was deaf? In the case of music, at least two senses are being accessed: we are *hearing* the music and we are also *feeling* it.

Strange as it seems, we can also *see* it. Recently I attended a symphony performing the work of Beethoven. As I closed my eyes to listen, I saw waves of multi-colored energy coming from the stage. I did not see this with my physical eyes, but experienced it through my emotional senses. Just as we can use more than one sense, we can also use more than one body.

If you have ever said, "It smells like fall," is it your sense of smell you are using, or a feeling, or both? What about when you say, "I see," in response to a comment someone has made? Your may be seeing it in your mind's eye, but you could also be feeling the image they are expressing to you. How about when someone says, "It left a bad taste in my mouth." Has she actually tasted it? How can this be?

The explanation lies in the fact that the physical body is linked to the subtle bodies through the glandular system. Each gland plays its role in connecting the bodies. For instance, the pineal gland is the link to our inner sight, and the amygdala is the gateway to emotional trauma. The bodies cannot be separated for they all work together simultaneously.

This is an important fact to keep in mind when doing your clearing work, because each event that has taken place in your life has affected all your bodies. It works the same way when clearing these events. When you move energy in one body, it also moves in the others. So no matter what level you choose to work from, you are actually working in all bodies at the same time.

There may be times when it is easier, faster, and more effective to address the issue in one of the subtle bodies rather than the physical. Sometimes the reverse is true. There is no definitive course of action, as each situation is unique.

The Supra-physical Body

The supra-physical body is a grid system or matrix that overlays the physical. Problems don't usually originate here. Beginning in the other bodies, they travel through this one on the way to the physical. The way you might have experienced this is by *feeling* you are coming down with a cold, yet you have none of the physical symptoms.

When negative thinking or emotions have worked their way into the supra-physical body, but have not yet manifested into the physical, it can be detected by the subtle senses but probably will not show up on any medical test. You are sensing an energetic imbalance that is too subtle for detection with the instruments presently available.

Since the equipment used in diagnosis is incapable of measuring the condition, it is hard for doctors to determine what is wrong and they may send you home saying you are in good health. It is possible for disease to remain in the supra-physical body for years before it manifests into the physical. However, if it is invasive enough and left untreated, the condition will eventually make its way into the physical body.

Scientists have documented physiological and emotional changes in plants and animals using a technique called Kirlian photography. This method captures on a photographic plate what is purported to be an aura of energy that emanates from an object. Using this method, they have seen that as a plant is getting ready to grow a new leaf, there is a matrix of energy that appears around the branch. This develops and fills in before the leaf appears in physical form. That matrix is the plant's supra-physical body.

Keeping the subtle bodies healthy goes a long way towards ensuring better health in the physical. Most disease begins in the subtle bodies as hurt, fear, shame, hatred, trauma, anger, guilt, etc. If nothing is done to clear the thought or emotion from the body where it originates, it will harden and eventually work its way into the supra-physical body. It won't be long until it moves into the physical.

By the time symptoms manifest in the physical body, the causes have been lurking in the inner bodies for awhile. It is easier and faster to clear things before they reach the more solid physical state, because once they do, they will have to be physically treated or allowed to run their course.

The clearing work releases destructive energies while still in etheric form, so they don't have a chance to reach the physical body. However, even if physical manifestation has already occurred, this work will help since working in one body, affects all the others.

The Emotional Body

The emotional body is the seat of emotions. This is a most wondrous part of our makeup. From emotions, we create, feel and connect with Divine Source God. This sets us apart from other beings, as many do not have emotional bodies.

The emotional body is the sensitive part of you. It is able to pick up nuances in things people say and do. You then interpret the words or actions as hostile, loving, angry, etc. based on how you feel. The accuracy with which you interpret these feelings depends on how clear the emotional body is.

In this country, we are taught that emotions are harmful, destructive, and bad, so we learn early in life to suppress them. The television, movies, and video games show us such horrendous things that we shut down our emotional bodies and become desensitized. We also push our emotions away to keep from experiencing pain. The rampant use of drugs and alcohol sedates, twists and destroys the emotional body.

When the emotional body is sick and out of balance, we become numb or else overreact to everything that comes up in life. This can be quite inconvenient, so the mental body steps in and suppresses the emotional body. This can create even more long-term issues because we then respond from a state of pure logic. In our western world, this is accepted, and even encouraged, but it is less than ideal in the bigger picture because things get totally out of balance. In order to have stability on our planet and in our lives, we need all of the bodies healthy and performing the role they were designed to play.

Experiencing emotion is a great gift, yet there appears to be a movement to rid our race of them. Those in power on this planet would like nothing better than for us to suppress our emotions because when we repress our feelings, they fold in on us causing fear, guilt, depression, shame, anger, and hatred. This destroys our self-worth. Swimming in the soup of these negative emotions keeps us down and easily controlled. It is imperative for us to have a healthy emotional body, as it is our bridge to Divine Source God and our sovereignty.

The Memory Body

The memory body is where our memories and history are stored—it is the home of our past. It holds an account of everything we have ever experienced. It is the seed for life's experiences. This storehouse of information influences our reasoning and everything we do.

For instance, if a child tries to receive love and hugs from his parents and is continually pushed away, if he is made promises that are never kept, and if he is talked to as if he were the worst kid in the world, he stores the event along with whatever he was feeling at the time. He may forget that these things happened to him, but they and the emotions he felt at that time are still stored inside and they influence the choices he makes.

Perhaps, later in life he falls in love with a woman, yet he can't give her the affection he would dearly love to give. She says she loves him and wants to be with him, but he has a hard time believing she will follow through on her promises, so he can't commit to a relationship with her. He puts himself down before anyone else has a chance—somehow that hurts less.

His past experiences are causing him to unconsciously sabotage things today, because he doesn't want to set himself up for a fall. Consciously he may have no idea why things won't work, but it doesn't matter whether it makes sense. The memory body has it all recorded in detail and is playing out the scenario over and over, influencing his life regardless of whether he remembers or not.

The problem with making decisions based on stored memories is that you are not the same person you used to be and your life circumstances may have also changed. You are evolving with each experience you have, so your decisions must reflect that in order to keep moving forward. A solution based on outdated information may prove to be inappropriate. This can also cause you to act out of fear and keep you attracting the same unwanted things into your life.

People who don't realize that things change often live through the past. They are caught up in their memory body. You will know them because they keep repeating the same dissatisfying, destructive choices, never seeing there is any other way. Their conversation becomes dull and boring as they relate over and over things that happened to them throughout their life. They may slide from one event to another or get hung up on one time period from which they often have great difficulty extricating themselves. They are not present in the here and now and all life is based on what once was. This keeps them in a loop of experience that is old and worn out, and there is no empowerment in taking this approach to life.

The memory body does not have to be an anchor around your ankle. You can use it to help you in your journey through life. Through it you can look at your past and see where you can make changes, then set your course in a new direction. In that way you gain wisdom from your experiences and are free to release them to go on to new ones.

The Mental Body

The mental body is the home of logic, thoughts, mental processes, and understanding. It is where philosophy and religion reside. It is the "Spock" part of our makeup.

This body uses past experiences and things you have learned to reason out answers to your questions. It is a great tool for gathering information, balancing the checkbook, reading a map, and setting up a new sound system, but perhaps not as efficient when it comes to solving relationship problems, having compassion for a sick friend, or experiencing the pleasure of a bubble bath.

There is no heart or compassion in decisions made from this level. The mental body's choices are based strictly on logic. It was designed to help us in many situations, but it was not meant to operate without the assistance of the other bodies. We need all of the bodies working together to maintain balance and make decisions that will serve our needs and that of others.

Western society is primarily a mental culture. Use of the mental body is strongly encouraged in the decision making process. We are taught to make decisions and act solely from logic. If we can justify the logic in why we did something or show a precedence written somewhere, chances are those in authority will not hold us accountable. Using only logic to make decisions puts the mental body in a position of carrying a burden that should be shared by all of our bodies. As a result, things get out of balance. We become stressed, shut down or sick.

The mental body has thoughts passing through it continuously; some are uplifting and some are destructive. These thoughts seem to just be "out there" and they pass through us on their way to some unknown destination. There is no energy in them until we put it there. We do this by giving them our attention. Attention is the magnifier that causes them to grow. We create with each thought we entertain. So in order to manifest the things we want and avoid that which we don't want, it becomes crucial to focus on thoughts that support our goals.

The Unconscious Body

The unconscious body has several parts. It is made up of the subconscious, superconscious, instinct, and intuition. There is no reasoning here, it accepts whatever it is given so we have little conscious control over this body. It is where tapes are stored, the "shoulds," "can'ts" and "musts." The unconscious body stores the subjective side of our experiences. You may not be aware of what is stored in this body, but it is influencing you just the same.

The unconscious body is like a computer, and if you find yourself repeating a behavior that you want to change, you have to reprogram this part of you. You can either update what is already there or change it altogether by using the Releasing Negative Energy Affirmation found in Chapter 8.

The Spiritual Body

The spiritual body is the vehicle for experience beyond time and space. It can see the bigger picture because it is not subject to the polarities the other bodies experience.

When operating from this level, we can make more in-
formed choices. We *are* freedom.

How The Bodies Interact

The bodies all have a role to play. As long as each is
taking care of its responsibilities, life goes along fairly
smoothly.

When a decision needs to be made, the bodies give
their opinions, and a decision is easily reached if they all
agree. A problem arises when they do not agree on a course
of action. This is why it can be difficult to determine what
to do. If one of the bodies wants something and feels it *has*
to have it, it may choose to disregard the opinions of the
other bodies. More discussion may follow until your
strongest body says, "Just do it." At that point, it is a done
deal.

One would think that the bodies would have a well-
defined interaction that results in decisions that always
serve our best interest. Possible, but not probable. Unfortunately, all the programs the bodies have accumulated
throughout our lifetime will come forward, causing conflict.
The decisions that are reached are not necessarily serving
our highest good. The *programs* have no interest in our
welfare, only in protecting their agenda.

Battles are fought between the bodies for many reasons. One body may feel that another one is not doing its job well enough so it steps in and takes charge. This is quite often the mental body, since mental functions are the ones most strongly supported in our culture. When this happens, it is only a matter of time before the controlling body experiences burnout.

Conflicts between the bodies can cause confusion, indecision, depression, and loss of power. To overcome this, it is necessary to get the bodies communicating and working together.

The bodies will do what they must to protect themselves from these conflicts. One may put a suit of armor around itself, lash out, or shut down. If this happens often enough, damage can be done to the assaulted body.

Danielle was an incredible business-woman. She knew how to get things done and people liked her. She never got angry and always had a smile. When she first came to me, I checked in with each of her bodies and saw that the emotional body was in great pain. It looked like it wanted to burst into tears, but there was no way she could allow that. It was filled with dark gooey stuff, representing the fear, pain, and anger she felt as the result of things that had happened to her. Its heart had a clamp around it to hold it together.

After she got her pieces back, the spiritual surgeons repaired her heart chakra. They started it pumping energy and reconnected the broken circuitry. Energy flowed into the heart chakra, solar plexus, and root chakra. We discussed ways she could nurture herself. The third eye was covered and not able to give input to the mental so the spiritual surgeons removed the covering that had grown over it. They worked on the core of the emotional body.

The mental body appeared to be on steroids, which it needed to keep up the pace as it was doing the work of the emotional body as well as its own. We dialogued with it and it said it did not trust the emotional body, so it had to do everything itself. We explained to the mental body that it could now give up its hold and the emotional body would help it carry the load. It was not so sure and wanted some guarantee. Since there are no guarantees, we asked it to give it a try—what did it

have to lose? It accepted that and let the
work progress.

Sleuthing

Because the bodies all influence each other, don't always look to the physical body to find the cause of a physical problem. It may have started in one of the other bodies, and worked its way through to the physical body. Something couldn't get your attention, so it festered until it created a situation that was so uncomfortable it could no longer be ignored.

The original blockage could be in any of the bodies. Although it is not necessary, recognizing where the problem began can be of help in clearing the energy around it. Rosey is an example of someone whose memory body, working with the unconscious body, was creating unnecessary demands on her.

> *Rosey wanted some direction in her life.*
> *She was working two full-time jobs and*
> *was considering going to nursing school.*
> *She was a very responsible person and*
> *had been juggling many things in life. She*
> *was afraid if she went to school she would*
> *not be able to maintain the delicate bal-*

ance she had in her structured life. Her upbringing demanded that she maintain it despite the added responsibilities. She wanted to better her life, but how could she do it all?

When she was growing up, her father was the principal at her school so she always had to toe the line. She lived with many "shoulds," "have-to's" and "can'ts." She was not allowed to make excuses or to express herself in any way that he did not approve. There was always the pressure of, "What will the neighbors think?" Her memory body had learned well how to get along and succeed in this environment. It got her through her childhood, but it was holding her back now.

The training she had received was well programmed into her memory body, but there was a nine-year-old part of her that still knew how to have fun. We asked that part to come forward to help her remember there were other ways of dealing with life. Together she and her child part brought forth memories and the realization that she did not have to give up one for the other. She was then able to see

*how she could work it out to go to school,
let go of the things that were not necessary and keep up with the things that were
important. When the "shoulds" were removed, her vision was clear.*

It takes a good detective to trace the problem back to the source. Where did it originate—in the physical, emotional, memory, mental body, or unconscious body? It is easier and more effective to clear the situation at its origination point than the last place it manifested, though that body may need some attention as well.

In order to find the origination point, you can scan the bodies. Pay attention to what you feel and the thoughts that come. You don't have to struggle or try to force anything— just be the observer. If you don't see or feel anything, it is okay. Just proceed with one of the clearing exercises and intend it will work as needed.

Exercise: Determining the Point of Origin

Get comfortable. Lie down if you want. Set the space as discussed in Chapter 4. Surround yourself in the light. Invite in the light and sound, your teachers, guides, divine self, and anyone who will work with you for your best and highest good.

Starting at the top of your head, move your attention down your body. As you do, look for dark spots, sounds that are off key, energy waves that are fluctuating at strange frequencies, murky colors, anything that does not feel like the rest of you.

If you are a tactile person, you will sense areas where something just doesn't feel right. Perhaps you feel it as stuck energy. If vision is your dominant sense, you may see spots, clouds, or objects. If hearing is your strongest sense, you might hear a change in frequency. It might sound like a beautiful symphony playing as you travel through your body, and then you hear a sour note. If smell is the major sense through which you experience, you might become aware of a toxic odor. If using taste, you may get something like a metallic sensation in your mouth.

Move your attention down the body to the throat, shoulders, left arm into the hand, right arm into the hand, down the torso, visualizing the organs as you go. Proceed down the left leg to the knee, ankle, and foot. Move down the right leg to the knee, ankle, and foot.

Once you have located an area in distress, bring rainbow colors of light into the area of your body where you located the imbalance. Intend that it filter through all of your bodies. If you hear a tone inside your head, see if you can reproduce it with your voice. If you are unable to see the light or hear a sound, just intend that the light and whatever tone is best for you come into that area. As you do this, feel what happens. Continue this procedure with each area where you find a disturbance.

When you finish, intend that the work become part of your reality in the best way possible for you and that it all be done with ease and grace. Congratulate and thank yourself for all the good work you have done.

Comments on Results

The above exercise may seem like a simple thing to do or it may be quite foreign to you. Even if you are not aware of anything happening, you might be surprised at the wonderful changes you feel in your bodies after doing it a few times. The following are some comments from others who have tried this exercise. They show the difference between experiencing through feeling and visual perceptions.

> *"I guess overall I started off feeling everything felt fine as I went down. Then I felt a little twinge in the right knee, very minor, but when I put the light there, the pain just faded and was gone."*

* * *

"I have been working on old issues the last month and they were just kind of stored all over the place. I didn't find anything too major. Nothing major like, 'oh my God' stuff. They dissolved and went away when I shined the light on them. They had manifested into the physical from the emotional."

* * *

"I am real visual. I had three black spots. I put light in there and that did it. The darkness just rolled out like a fog."

Other Ideas

The subtle bodies play a huge role in the health and well-being of the physical body. If you clear them regularly using this simple exercise, you are emptying your backpack and freeing yourself of the energies that weaken your immune system, cause illness, and wreak havoc in your life.

Chapter 6
The Chakras

You are a perfect yet expanding being in a perfect yet expanding world in a perfect yet expanding universe.

Esther and Jerry Hicks
Ask And It Is Given

Guidelines Only

The logical mind likes things laid out nice and neat, but not all things are. In talking about the chakras, we can discuss similarities that are found from person to person, but not all people follow the textbook description of how chakras should look and act.

One person I talked with said she saw her chakras in rings around her body. I had never thought about that, but as soon as she said it, I could see what she meant. Our chakras may be varying shades and tones of colors. There may also be more than one color found in a chakra. This can happen for a number of reasons. The chakra may need to be cleaned. It could be using the energy of another color to clear, balance, or enhance it. It could also be normal for the individual. The logical mind wants to categorize things, so it is easiest to use the norm as a guideline; but don't let this picture lock you into a view that this is how things HAVE to be.

Wheels of Light

Chakra is a Sanskrit word meaning "Wheel of Light." The physical, supra-physical, emotional, memory, mental, unconscious, and spiritual bodies each have their own set of chakras. The bodies are connected through the chakra systems and the glands. There are many other chakras throughout the bodies, but here we will address the seven main ones.

The chakras can be likened to computer centers for the bodies. They regulate the flow of energy in and out of the body. They open and close depending on mood, the people you are with, and what you are experiencing. For example, in a crowd your chakras may close somewhat to protect you from the many different energies surrounding you. But when you see a baby smile, they open.

The chakras are made up of filaments that form a cone shape, which allows them to act much like little tornadoes. They breathe in through their center and out on the outer edges. The opening of the chakra is about the size of an orange. This is considered normal but the size of the opening can vary depending on the person and circumstances. The small end of the cone hooks into the core, an energetic corridor or tunnel traversing through the center of each body. The core for each body is like the spine in the physical body. Each chakra is composed of a front and back with the exception of the root and crown. The root chakra extends into the earth and the crown is our connection with the etheric.

If a chakra is damaged, the body's innate intelligence will reroute that chakra's energy flow to the others. The other chakras will attempt to compensate, but since they were not designed to do another chakra's work, they are usually a poor substitute for the damaged one.

The chakras govern different parts of the body; i.e., the lower back is affected by what is going on in the sacral chakra. If pain is in the tailbone, chances are the root chakra is involved. If you are having problems with the stomach or digestion, something may be malfunctioning in your solar plexus chakra.

The chakras work together to form an aura around the body; some call it the electromagnetic field. The aura remains stable for the most part, but will fluctuate with whatever you are experiencing. If this field is not strong, you can attract lower vibrational experiences and people into your life. Since the chakras determine the strength of your electromagnetic field, it is important that you keep them clear and operating in harmony.

Your energetic field not only affects you but those around you, just as you are affected by other peoples' fields. You may not be able to consciously see another's aura, but you feel it. It can leave you feeling weak in the stomach, happy to be with them, or wanting to run from them.

Sick Chakras

When a chakra is "sick," it can take on a misshapen form, it can be pulled in on itself or be elongated. The color can be muddy, pieces can be missing, or filaments can be broken. It can feel cool or hot if you place your hand over that part of the body. It can be shut down, spinning off balance, or it may appear flat.

If you feel threatened, angry, hurt, or stressed, you tend to close your chakras by making their opening smaller. This may be necessary for your protection in that moment, but if they remain blocked or closed for extended periods, it could result in illness to the body where this is occurring. If the energy does not move through the chakra, the chakra fills up with energy that becomes stagnant, blocking the flow through that part of the system. Therefore, it is important they be open in order to maintain good health.

Sometimes chakras are used to store symbols or images you want to keep close to you. These things do not belong in the chakras, as it prevents them from spinning correctly like a washing machine spinning out of balance.

Simon was a devout Christian. He prayed to Jesus every day and lived the best life he could. He had a pain in his heart that would not go away. In an etheric clearing, we found he had placed a crucifix in his heart. Simon loved Jesus and wanted to share in his suffering, so he placed the cross there.

If left, the cross could eventually have caused a heart condition for him, as he was interrupting the flow of energy. We talked about other ways he could connect with Jesus. Once we found one that

*worked for him, he released the cross and
his pain dissipated.*

The Root Chakra

The root chakra is connected to the core at the base of the spine. When healthy, this chakra is a beautiful shade of red—the color of life, warmth, and passion. The exact shade and hue varies somewhat from person to person. It reflects your will to live. This chakra governs your well being, feeling of safety, stability and connection to the earth. It pulls the energy of the earth up into you to keep you nurtured and energized, and carries energy from you to the earth. This back and forth action is ongoing, feeding and cleansing the bodies.

When you get frightened, this chakra often pulls up and in, so it is no longer solidly connected to the earth. This is reflected in your breathing too. You inhale and neglect to fully exhale; it is like you are holding your breath. When this chakra is not connected you feel vulnerable.

If the root chakra is out of balance, you can experience anger, insecurity, greed, imbalance, or suicidal feelings. Physical illness can be caused by a weak root chakra and a poor connection with the earth because you are not getting the energy into the body.

Sometimes there is an energy leak in this chakra, much like a garden soaker hose. This was the case with Ellen.

> *Ellen had been seriously ill. She had a meeting scheduled with a prominent person and very much wanted to be ready for it energetically. In looking at her chakras, we found that the root chakra was not connecting properly with the earth.*
>
> *Four of Ellen's friends had been sick and were having problems. Through her love and desire to help them, she had allowed them to tap into her energy flow, which was causing a poor connection between her and the earth. This was draining her energy. The spiritual surgeons removed the ties these people had inserted into her and we asked her friends' guides to help them. Then the surgeons repaired the holes in her root chakra, which helped her feel physically better and more confident regarding her meeting.*

The Sacral Chakra

The sacral chakra is located a few inches below the navel and resonates with the color orange. Orange carries the vibration of vitality and energy. It governs the sexual organs, sensual expression, creativity, flexibility, physical strength, how you fit into the world, and your ability to experience pleasure. It determines how well you manifest in the physical reality. This chakra is very closely related to the root chakra and some of their functions overlap.

If this chakra is not in balance it can cause competition, laziness, shame, holding back in life, not being able to create the life you want, masochism, and lying. Some of these characteristics stem from other chakras too, but they are basic to this chakra.

Ted's company was going through a layoff. He liked his job, so when the company offered to transfer him to another location, he decided to relocate his family. Once he started working in the new office, he realized how badly that branch of the company was run. Ted was discouraged and quit the job. He put off finding another job because what he really wanted to do was work in the area of alternative healing.

The first thing his body said was, "Why bother? No one wants what I have to offer." His sacral chakra said, "It *doesn't matter what I want; I can't have it anyway." The creativity in the sacral chakra was being stifled because that chakra was not connected properly to the solar plexus (power center) or the throat chakra (point of manifestation). So he had the ideas, but couldn't express it into the world. The spiritual surgeons cleared the chakras, got them connected and working together.*

The sacral chakra is very bright in some people and dull in others. Neither is desired if you want to be in balance. If this chakra is dim, there is not enough energy flowing through it and the person will probably not feel much energy, ability to manifest, creativity, or sensuality. If it is consistently bigger and brighter than the other chakras, it has more energy running through it than the others and could end up in burn-out. Perhaps you have felt someone sexually drawing on your energy, pulling you toward him or her; this is called sexual magnetism. This person is using the sacral chakra to do this.

In this country, one of the greatest areas of learning is in sexuality, as people seem to have many sexual hang-ups and perversions. There is powerful energy in this chakra. When you learn to use it instead of allowing it to use you, a wonderful storehouse of energy becomes available for manifesting your dreams.

The Solar Plexus Chakra

The solar plexus chakra is located at the base of the ribs. It is yellow in color, which is a happy and uplifting color. This chakra has to do with your will. It affects your personal power, laughter, self-control, prejudice, fear, and transformation. Its health determines how empowered you are. Clues that this chakra is wounded are seen in a person who is the victim or in one who tries to control or manipulate others.

Georgia wanted to do her work but felt she needed a partner to help. She wanted to get going on the work so badly that she was willing to sacrifice her integrity. Because of this she attracted people who took advantage of her. We looked at why this was happening.

In the solar plexus we found betrayal. She had worked for a company on a project that someone sabotaged. No one knew it was her competitor who sabotaged it—they just thought it failed. Because it "failed," the funding was pulled. Georgia found out about the sabotage but couldn't prove it. She harbored hatred towards those involved. She felt betrayed.

She had known the project had a high potential to be used in a destructive manner but didn't care because she wanted recognition for working on such a high profile project. She did nothing to stop it or build safeguards into it, and her guilt opened the door to the sabotage and betrayal by her competitor. She lost her power and this put her in the position of being the victim in the deals she had tried to work out after that.

By clearing this, she was able to later bring in a partner that was sincere and had high integrity.

Keeping your power center clear is most important. You will not have to take power from someone else if this chakra is clear and flowing energy freely. You will have enough of your own. It is only when you try to take it from someone else that you become manipulative and your actions destructive.

The Heart Chakra

The heart chakra is in the middle of the chest and is green in color. Green is the color of balance and harmony. This chakra influences your ability to give and receive love, forgiveness, peace, acceptance, and compassion. It is the connecting point between the three lower and the three upper chakras. It brings together your heaven and your earth.

It is the seat of the divine part of you, which is your connection to Divine Source God. If you feel you don't have a strong connection with Divine Source God, it could be because you have built walls around the heart. You can't make a strong connection when the heart chakra isn't operating openly in a healthy manner.

> *Jackson was graduating from college and was at a crossroads in life. His lower three chakras were in good shape, but the heart was not connecting with his divine self because of beliefs and expectations. This was keeping him from having joy in his life. Although he had much to celebrate in his life, he could not allow himself to take a breath and enjoy his successes.*
>
> *The spiritual surgeons worked to help him change those beliefs and to balance*

*the part that was so serious. His guides
showed him it was okay to have fun. After
this, he relocated and started his own
business. Once he was able to relax and
connect to his divine self, his life got even
better.*

The Throat Chakra

The throat chakra is at the base of the throat just above
the collarbone and is blue in color. Blue is associated with
serenity, relaxing, and soothing. The throat chakra's state of
health determines how well you can speak up for yourself,
ask to have your needs met and express the truth coming
from your power center. It is about your honesty, discernment, writing, and expressing your uniqueness to the world
through words, actions, feelings, and thoughts.

The throat often becomes plugged with choked-back
words, screams, tears, pain, and energy plugs that you put
in to stop you from speaking or doing things that you know
won't gain you approval. In order to keep this chakra
healthy, it is important that you begin doing what is yours
to do and speaking your words of truth in a loving manner.
In the case with Denise, her throat chakra definitely needed

some help, but her other chakras also played a role in creating a situation in her life.

Denise was getting psychic messages, but was hesitant to share the messages Spirit was giving her. She told herself it was okay to express the messages and allow others to see that part of her, but she was still stopping herself. She felt she had one foot nailed to the floor and was walking in circles.

The throat chakra was the main one affected because she could not speak her truth, but the other chakras also contributed to her situation. Her root chakra would not ground. The sacral chakra was crying. It said it had no place on this planet and that it was not safe to be herself. The solar plexus said, "They blame me for everything." The heart chakra was crying because Denise could not sing her song. The brow chakra was anxious. The crown said it didn't want to be too public.

Years before she had given uninvited information to someone who considered it to be lies, so she was punished. And she was still paying the price. Her power ani-

mals collected the pieces of the power she had lost, she apologized to the person she had upset, and her guides connected her to her life contract.

Denise had made some mistakes and was punished. Since she did not want to repeat that experience, she shut down the gifts she had. She tried to ignore them, but was not happy because she was not expressing her uniqueness. Once the pattern was cleared, she was able to begin opening to share her gifts in healthy ways.

The Brow Chakra

The brow chakra is located just above the eyebrows in the middle of the forehead and is indigo in color. Indigo is the color of deep inner vision. Its state of health determines your clairvoyance and ability to visualize, sense, and hear what is not apparent to your physical senses.

This chakra often becomes cluttered with thoughts, beliefs, attitudes, and habits that cloud your thinking and perspective. This is like wearing many different pairs of glasses, creating distortion in how you view the world and what happens to you.

Elizabeth was diagnosed with cancer. It came as a shock because she had not been ill. She went in for her annual exam and it was discovered through the blood test. She was determined to heal herself and did much research on the web. She talked to the medical doctors and alternative health practitioners. She knew the disease was only part of the equation and that her thoughts and feelings also determined her fate.

After she gathered the medical and alternative information, she decided to go with standard medical procedures, but to also work with alternative therapies. Her doctor approved the program she set up but did not believe any of it would make any difference, because his professional opinion was that she would be dead in three weeks.

Every day Elizabeth faithfully followed the protocol she had come up with. She went to the cancer clinic for weekly tests and shots. She took the herbs prescribed for her. She had Reiki, reflexology, and massage treatments. She did etheric clearing. She did gentle workouts. She talked to her cells about what they needed to do to heal the body. She visualized the "good" cells winning.

Elizabeth was doing a great job and her body was holding its own, but her brow chakra was being overwhelmed by having to manage everything.

Her guides suggested she make a tape with affirmations on it. She could play the tape as she fell asleep at night and when she took her rest in the afternoon. This would allow her to rest and at the same time make sure she covered all the bases. After doing this, the brow chakra released the feeling of being over-whelmed. It was as if the chakra opened up and took a deep breath.

Elizabeth got her affairs in order while doing everything else she wanted to do. She traveled, bought a motor home and camped, went to a conference, had great times with her family and friends, and watched lots of funny movies.

She extended her life well over a year beyond her doctor's three-week diagnosis. She was sometimes tired from the medical treatments she received, but she lived vir-

tually pain free. She left this life feeling complete.

The Crown Chakra

The crown chakra is located on the top of the head. It is the soft spot in infants. The color associated with this chakra is violet, the color of transmutation. It is your connection to your life contract and the cosmic energy. Your life contract is the agreement you made before entering into this physical body. It is a list of things you wanted to learn during your life.

When the crown is in balance you will feel inspiration, unity, and wisdom. When this chakra is blocked or damaged, you have a hard time knowing what your purpose and direction are in life. You also are not fully able to bring in the cosmic energy.

Tom had lived in Germany while in high school. He spoke fluent German and planned to go back there to live after graduation. He had many social and extra-curricular activities and rarely took time to replenish himself. He had to remain focused, and could never let himself take any down time. In looking at his crown chakra, we found that he kept repeating one part of his contract and would not move on to the next thing. He was stuck in a loop.

While living in Germany, he had an experience that was very traumatic for him. Although it was not his fault, he blamed himself. His life was focused on and structured around his returning to Germany to set things right. His guides were able to get the crown chakra to release this obsession and the need to repeat the pattern, so he could move on to other things.

The Core

In order to have health in the chakras and the bodies, the chakras must be able to act individually and also interact with one another. When things are working properly, they all pull energy in and breathe energy out. They also exchange energy through their connection via the core. The core acts much like the spine in our physical body in that it holds things together and furnishes a column through which energy can flow. In this way, the chakras are in constant communication and working together.

The core is made up of tiny filaments that carry light. These filaments can become damaged or clogged so that energy does not pass easily through them. At times the core kinks or twists and this causes blockages in the energy flow. This affects the whole system because the core needs to be cleared in order to have an unobstructed flow of energy through it.

When things are working properly, you bring energy in through the crown chakra, and it travels down the core and out the root chakra into the earth. The earth energy comes up through the root chakra, travels up the core and out the crown chakra into the cosmos. This flow keeps you stable and grounded in heaven and in earth.

The Chakras Interact Through the Core

No chakra is more important than the others. They are not separate, but work as a team, so they all need to be balanced and harmonized for everything to flow. If one is off-balance, another one has to carry its load. If one is enlarged and looks as if it has been on steroids, another chakra has been weakened.

Daisy is a potter who takes her work very seriously. Her life was falling apart.

When we looked at her chakras, the sacral was huge and dynamic while the rest of the chakras were drained. In an attempt to make lots of great pots, she was putting all of her time and energy into creatively working the clay. In the process, she had pulled energy from the other chakras into the sacral area. She was giving everything she had to her pottery but her health and life were paying the price.

The chakras are a team, and as with any team, each player is designed to play a specific role. The role is different for each. The heart chakra cannot play the role of the sacral, and the brow cannot play the role of the root. That would be like asking a liver to stand in for the heart, yet we often do this when one chakra is damaged and not functioning properly. It may get us through the crisis, but doing this puts stress on one, while causing the other to weaken.

It is important to have all the chakras working together, each doing what it was designed to do. Any chakra can interact with any other chakra. The following simplified example demonstrates how they interact, if all are doing their job efficiently.

The process for creating something in your lives goes like this: The crown chakra connects to your life contract. It reads the contract, and with your divine self determines what will be addressed. The brow chakra looks at it through its perspective and sends the information to the sacral chakra, which uses its creativity to determine how best to manifest the vision it is given. The root chakra gives it a reality check of what will and won't work in the physical, and it also pulls in the energy to support it. Once the sacral has the plan, it sends it to the solar plexus, which imbues it with the power to be manifested. Then it goes to the heart and that chakra checks to make sure it is in alignment with your highest good and gives it its blessing. Then it moves on to the throat where it is expressed or brought forth into form.

If there is damage in one of the chakras or the core, the creative process is thrown off track and either never reaches fruition or it comes through skewed. All chakras must be healthy and working together in harmony in order to receive and manifest the vision in the highest possible manner.

Exercise:
Technique for Clearing the Chakras

The basis for all energy work is intention, so it is important that you be clear in forming that intent. If you are choosing to work with another person, it is equally important that his or her intent for you be of the highest integrity.

I gave a client this exercise to do and when she came the next time, the front of her chakras were open and bright. I commented that she had really been working on herself, but asked what happened to the back of the chakras. She said, "Oh, I was supposed to do the back too?" The difference between the front and back of her chakras was amazing. The fronts were open and beautiful, while the backs were closed and muddy. So as you do this, intend that both the front and back of each chakra be addressed.

This exercise is one you may want to record on audiotape and play back during meditation or as you drift off to sleep. It is worth the time it takes, as you will feel relaxed and at ease.

This work is done through your intention—the most powerful tool you have when doing energy work. You can start at either the root chakra or the crown chakra, wherever feels best. In this example, we will start at the root.

At any point in this exercise, you may get a vision, word, or some indication of what has been happening in that part of your system. Just make a mental note of it. If nothing comes, don't worry and don't force anything to happen. It is still working.

Before beginning, set your space as described in Chapter 4.

As you know from basic science classes, white light is made up of all the color rays. You can use the white light in your work by bringing it to the root chakra. Then ask the red ray of that white light to go into that chakra and clean, clear, balance, and nurture it in all of the bodies (physical, supra-physical emotional, memory, mental, unconscious, and spiritual bodies). You may be aware that something is happening or you may feel nothing. Either way, it is okay. Just be open to the light and to releasing anything that is stored there that is not serving your highest good. Ask that this chakra extend into the earth, so it can bring energy up into you. You want a nice flow of energy from the earth to you.

Let that continue to work, as you use your intent to bring the white light up the core to the sacral chakra. Allow the orange ray of that white light to go into that chakra and clean, clear, balance, and nurture it front and back and in all of the bodies. Remember all of the chakras between the root and crown have a front and back to them. Pay attention to anything that comes to your awareness, but don't get hung up on it. If nothing seems to be happening, just pretend—a special type of *intending*—that you know how to do this and that wondrous things are taking place. Intention will cause it to be so.

Let that continue to work, as you bring the white light up the core to the solar plexus. Ask the yellow ray of that white light to go into that chakra and clean, clear, balance, and nurture it front and back and in all the bodies. Just relax and let the light and your intention do their work.

Next bring the light up to the heart chakra and ask the green ray to clean, clear, balance, and nurture that chakra front and back and in all the bodies. Relax and let go of anything that is blocking it. You can also release any barriers, walls or protective coverings you have placed around or in the heart. Feel it expanding and opening.

Let that continue to work, as you bring the light to the throat chakra. Ask the blue ray of the white light to clean, clear, balance, and nurture this chakra front and back and in all of the bodies. You may hear a sound or feel something. You may cough, tears may come up, whatever happens, just breathe deeply and let it release. Do not resist the energy flow or it becomes uncomfortable. Call in your guides or the spiritual surgeons if you need some help.

Let this continue to work and bring the white light to the brow chakra. Allow the indigo ray of the white light to go into the chakra and clean, clear, balance, and nurture it front and back and in all of the bodies. Let the old attitudes, perceptions, and beliefs fall from your inner eyes. Allow your inner hearing to open. Intend that you are freeing up anything that is stuck and blocking you in this chakra.

If you cannot see or feel this happening, just pretend you know how to do it and that it is taking place, and it will be so.

Let this continue to work and bring the light to the crown chakra. Allow the violet ray of the white light into this chakra and ask that it clean, clear, balance, and nurture this chakra front and back and in all of your bodies. Ask the light to feed the chakra and make it strong. As you release into the light anything that is no longer serving your highest good, see this light rise above you, connecting into the life force energy and bringing that energy down into your system.

Next ask that the light coming up the core clean the debris, clear any stuck energies, straighten the kinks and nurture the core. Ask that all the chakras be securely fastened into it so all are exchanging energy in whatever way is perfect and right for you. Allow the energy to flow in the top of the head, down through all of your bodies and out the root and into the earth. At the same time you bring energy from the earth up the core and out the top of the head. You now have energy freely flowing through your core and chakras.

The next step is to allow the clear energies that are flowing in the core and chakras to expand out into all parts of your bodies, nurturing them as well. Allow the energies to flow freely for a few minutes before jumping up to do whatever is next on your list for the day.

Hints for Using this Exercise

If visualization exercises are new to you and it is difficult to know what you are doing, trust that it is working because you have intended it so. Maybe you will feel sensations in the physical body. You may get hot or cold, feel pressure in your forehead, or your ears and face may become red and hot. This is due to increased energy. If it is too uncomfortable, ask for things to be regulated for you. Drinking more water throughout the day may also help it flow more easily.

During this exercise, you can relax and take a consciousness vacation or you can stay conscious and aware of what is happening in your subtle bodies. Neither way is better, as they both have benefits. In staying conscious, you can learn much about yourself, but be careful of trying to force things to happen.

When you do this exercise make sure the core is cleared as well as the chakras or the energy will not be able to move up and down between them like it needs to.

If you have trouble remembering the colors, just think of the rainbow, starting with the red at the root chakra. If you still can't remember the colors, intend that the light is flowing through the bodies and chakras in just the way that is right for you.

If you are short on time, you can do this exercise in the shower. As the water runs down over the body, intend that it is the light washing over, around, and through the core and chakras clearing and nurturing them.

Chakra Communication

It is well to understand the role of each of the chakras and what to look for when they are not working properly. With this information you can look to the chakras for information when things happen in your life. They can supply information as to where the problem is so you can repair it or clear the blockage. The chakras speak to you with their voice, color, size, shape, and spin. Once you become accustomed to this method of communication, it is easy to check on the health of your chakras.

Chapter 7
Reclaiming The Self

Whether you believe you can do a thing or not, you are right.

Henry Ford

Fragmentation

The idea that one can be fragmented or separated from the whole is an illusion many have bought into in this third density world. In truth there is no such thing as fragmentation; you are not broken, you don't have pieces missing, and you don't need to be fixed. However, since you may have accepted that you are, you have to treat your present situation as if it were real. We must work with things as they appear, because doing so helps us get to the point of realizing the deception.

Your natural state is wholeness, but in order to learn certain things while living on this earth, you allowed yourself to experience separation and fragmentation. In order to remember wholeness, you have to give up the idea that you are wounded and realize that separation is only an illusion you accepted as real.

If you look at the fragmentation program, you see that it is at work every day of your life. You give parts of yourself to your sweetheart, family, boss, the IRS, etc. You can also have parts of your power taken from you, or you may choose to put pieces aside if it is not safe to claim them. Whatever the cause, if too much of yourself is lost, you find you cannot live a balanced life. To reclaim your pieces and correct this situation, you can use the exercises at the end of this chapter.

Soul Retrieval

Soul retrieval is a phrase that originated with the ancient shamans, but in recent times, it has become a common phrase. It describes a technique whereby the shaman journeys in an altered state of consciousness outside of time and space to find a piece that has been lost, given away, or taken from the client who has come to them for assistance. The shaman brings the piece back and places it in the person. It oftentimes takes two to three months to integrate the replaced part. This technique has proven successful in helping a person come back into wholeness, but is a slow process and has to be done by the shaman.

In recent times, this procedure has been updated, allowing for multiple pieces to return at the same time and integration to occur usually within a 24-hour period. The process is so easy and simple that the retrieval can be done without depending on another to do it for you. You become a modern shaman in your own right.

Louise gave the following account of her reclaiming work and how she used it to help herself.

> *I felt emotionally drained and totally confused about my life. I was a grown woman and didn't seem to be able to cope. Then I did a retrieval. I had suffered in the abdominal area since I was 25 years old. After my mother passed away I experienced a great deal of anger, pain, guilt, and indecision about my feelings for her, so this clearing was to see what was going on and to get back anything I lost in that relationship.*
>
> *My mother and I had been at odds for some time and it appeared that we had sent destructive energies to one another through our thoughts and feelings. The intestinal problems were the result of a very piercing energy wound from my mother. With the use of intent and essential oils*

the wound was cleaned and cleared. I got back the pieces that were missing.

After this work, I was exhausted and slept most of the afternoon. My vision was changed and my pupils were small and stayed like that for about eight hours— evidently a symptom of the intense clearing.

After the work integrated, I felt like a new person. The problems I felt towards my mother were no longer there. I could now think of her in a loving light, realizing she did a good job teaching me the lesson of "what I didn't want to be." I miss her now and think of her lovingly, which is probably the first time in my life I felt that way.

It is a wonderful feeling to be whole and have love for my mother back all at the same time. All of it is due to the subtle body clearing I experienced. It changed my life.

Louise discovered the person she needed to work with didn't have to still be alive to clear the issues with her. This is true because the work is done outside time and space. She found that doing a retrieval left her feeling lighter, happier, and at peace. Others have found that relationships and health improve, fear dissipates, self-confidence and clarity return, and blockages dissolve.

The following story is more involved and I include it so you can see further possibilities with doing the reclaiming work.

> *Bonnie Rae had very little energy flowing through her body. It felt she was in the process of dying. She had just left her husband who had devoted his life to taking care of her physical needs, while ignoring her emotional needs. The right side of her body was not functioning well and she had difficulty walking.*
>
> *When she was seven years old her parents had separated and never told her why. On the day we did the work, her seven-year-old self was crying and walking alone in an area that looked like a bomb had exploded. A grown part of Bonnie Rae was in a cave where she had gone to die. They both felt that no one listened or cared what they thought. Their physical needs were met but not their emotional ones.*

*The right side of her body (the mascu-
line side) was not working because it was
overtaxed, especially since she was with-
drawing her energy from her body so she
could die. It also showed how heavily she
had relied on her husband (the masculine
side of her relationship). Meanwhile the
feminine side was off in the cave making
preparations to die. Her energies were
split. By bringing back the fragments her
parents and husband held and balancing
the masculine and feminine energies, she
regained her joy in living and her will to
live.*

*Many other parts were strewn about.
After gathering and returning them to the
child and the woman, the two came back
to present time and merged with Bonnie
Rae. This retrieval work left her feeling
empowered and ready for a better life.*

After reading this account you may feel there is no way
you could do this for yourself. When you begin the work,
you may not be aware of all these details, but I tell this
story so that you can see the possibilities you too can
achieve. As you work with the exercises in this book, similar things will be happening to you, but at first you may not

be conscious of the details. You will only know you feel better after doing them. And that is what is important.

Indications of Pieces Missing

Chances are everyone has spirit pieces missing. Here are some indicators that suggest this condition.

If you have experienced trauma, addiction, surgery, divorce, death of a loved one, abuse, military service, accidents, depression, memory gaps, have health issues, or have had a near death experience, there are probably pieces to reclaim.

If you have repeatedly put yourself into abusive situations and wonder why you keep making the same mistake, you probably have pieces to recover. If you argue with someone frequently, especially if it is the same argument over and over, there is cause to believe that one or both parties possess portions of the other. If you were to get back the fragments you lost, you would be able to break those repetitious patterns.

Saying things like, "A part of me left with him," "I just don't feel myself," "I gave everything to her and still she doesn't appreciate me," or "My heart is broken," is a good indication that something has been taken or given away. Reclaiming parts of self will truly help.

Rose put her baby up for adoption when she was a young girl. The baby was taken away as soon as it was born, so she didn't even get to say good-bye to the child she had carried for nine months. She was told it was better that way.

She and her daughter were reunited when the child was grown, but the trauma of the separation was still with her. She said she felt like her heart was broken. Energetically, her heart was broken and her solar plexus was wrapped in a cocoon. As the spiritual surgeons worked with her, the cocoon gently melted and she was given time with the baby. There was so much joy that it pushed the pain out. She reclaimed pieces from the father and the people involved in that event.

Rose saw snatches of the child's life she had missed and after this experience, her heart and solar plexus chakras were whole. She felt happy, fulfilled, and grateful.

When Rose said she felt her heart was broken, she was really speaking of her emotional heart center. Paying attention to the words we use to describe our feelings can be most beneficial, as they are oftentimes accurate metaphors for what we are experiencing.

Filling the Emptiness

Not being able to access parts of self causes pain, so people move quickly to try to balance the upset. Not wanting or not knowing *how* to deal with the pain may lead them to find someone else whose electro-magnetic field is weak and take her power. This is done by goading her into guilt, fear, anger, or shame. When a person can be made to feel these negative emotions, she is easily manipulated and controlled.

Another way to get energy is to put energy cords into another and siphon her energy when it is needed, kind of like sipping on a soft drink or coffee when energy is low.

People are very creative beings. If stealing the energy from another isn't possible or satisfying enough, they may choose to escape into drugs, gambling, alcohol, compulsive sex, obsessive shopping, or uncontrollable eating.

The true way to fill the void in self is to get in touch with your own power pieces. Then you no longer need to fill your emptiness with unsatisfying or artificial means.

Universal Effects of Fragment Integration

When you start getting back in touch with your power pieces, you are willing to give back the pieces you took from others. This allows *them* to return things they have taken from others, starting a chain reaction where clearing occurs for all.

As you do your own personal reclaiming work and come into wholeness, so do the people around you. Everything you do affects everyone around you and it even expands out into the universe. Likewise, what others experience affects us. This is true because we are all part of the oneness. We share a unity of purpose, so one can't happen without the other.

When you think of being part of the oneness, the Borg in "Star Trek" may come to mind. With the Borg, all were assimilated into one mind and all individuality was erased—all became part of a hive mentality. This is not the oneness a modern shaman is heading toward. In the true sense of the word, you are complete within yourself, and yet you are an integrated part of the whole system. You retain your individuality, while remaining connected to all life.

People have been taught to live a life of separation, but it is time to end this. Humans want so much to connect with each other, but deny that connection because they have been taught—especially in the west—to value individuality so fiercely. Hardly any recognition that there is a state of oneness to be entered into remains. Even those who do see the bigger picture may find it difficult to know how they fit into it.

Think what it would be like to live every day connected to oneness! You would never feel alone again. You would never want to hurt another. There would be no fear. The journey of separation has taken us as far as it can. It is time we come back to oneness.

"This sounds great," you say, "but how do I do this?" The first thing is to begin making changes within self. The techniques that follow were designed to assist you in reclaiming the pieces of self that you have "lost" in this world of illusion. Once you see there is no separation or fragmentation, you can slip right into the whole. When you do the exercises, they will help you get in touch with all that is rightfully yours.

Two Important Steps

In the following exercise, there are two steps that seem quite insignificant, but should never be skipped. Whether you do them or not will determine the success you have. These steps will decrease the time it takes to process the pieces and will make it much easier for you to integrate them. The shamans of old did not include these steps. That is why their way of working was slow and oftentimes painful.

In the traditional shamanic practice of soul retrieval, the shaman would find the missing part, bring it back and put it into the person. During the time it was gone, the person had changed, so the piece no longer vibrated at his frequency. If it was sad, mad, or fearful when it left, that is how it returned; and, when replaced, those emotions had to be dealt with. If another person was in possession of the piece, the piece took on his vibration and was no longer harmonious with the owner. These things cause the integration to be more difficult and time consuming.

The solution is to change the vibration of the returning piece so it is harmonious. You can do this before bringing it in. It is simple to use intention to clean the piece and change its vibrations to match your own. By using the process described in the following exercise, you can restore multiple pieces simultaneously with very little time or energy required for integration.

The second step you will want to be sure to take is to let *the light* integrate all the work and pieces once you get them back. Doing this smoothes the integration.

You can think of yourself as a three dimensional puzzle. When a piece is gone, the edges get rough so when the piece comes back, it doesn't fit exactly. Taking the following simple approach eliminates having any problems with the returning part.

Exercise:
Reclaiming the Self – The Fountain

The following technique was designed to assist in simply and easily reclaiming your pieces. It will help you gather that which is rightfully yours, thereby helping you remember and connecting you with oneness.

This exercise is so simple you can do it every day. You don't have to see or hear anything, although you will likely feel stronger, lighter, and more peaceful when you finish. There is empowerment in being able to identify the pieces that come back, but it is not necessary because this work is based on your intention.

Get comfortable. Send your root chakra into the earth to ground and stabilize you. It will spread out like roots of a tree giving you a firm foundation from which to work. Allow yourself to sink into a quiet space protected by the forces of light.

Intend or feel yourself standing in a pool of liquid light. It looks like water, but really it is liquid light. It may be golden in color, but it could be any color. Just notice what you can about it. How does it make you feel?

Once you are comfortable in the light, use your intention to call into the fountain anything you are ready to get back. These pieces can come from any time, any place, or anyone. Only those things that belong to you can enter this pool. You may be able to identify them, they may feel like energy, or perhaps you feel and see nothing at all. It does not matter, as your intent is working for you. Do not be concerned if the pieces are dirty or broken; accept them into the fountain just as they are.

As these things come into the fountain of light, allow the liquid light to wash over and through the items and you, cleaning them and you until all are crystal clear and they are matched to your vibration.

You may have a feeling that the work is finished or you may not. In either case, just intend that once the pieces are harmonious to you and matched to your vibration, they enter into you in just the right way. You don't have to know how to do this; the pieces know where they belong. So just intend it be done in accordance with your highest good.

You may feel a loving warmth go through your body as this happens, but if you don't feel anything don't worry. You didn't do it wrong. Trust that whatever needed to happen did. Welcome the parts back.

Thank the person for returning the piece to you and invite him to go into his own fountain for clearing. See a golden light flow down through your body integrating the pieces you have reclaimed. Thank them for coming back to you. Thank yourself for allowing them to return.

And thank your guides and divine self for
their help.

You may do this exercise with any trauma, such as a
car accident, "killer exam," job loss, relocation, or surgery.
It also works with things such as overly graphic movies,
school, government agencies, church, jobs, or hospital vis-
its. Any time you have an experience that troubles you, reclaim the pieces from which you disconnected. No doubt
you lost something in the process.

Exercise:
Reclaiming the Self – Journal Writing

If you want to get more in-depth with your reclaiming
work, you can do some writing to get clarity.

Get comfortable. Send your root
chakra into the earth to ground and stabilize you. It will spread out like roots of a
tree giving you a firm foundation from
which to work. Allow yourself to sink into a
quiet space protected by the forces of
light.

Once you are comfortable and in a
safe space, make a list of everyone you
feel has mistreated you or to whom you

feel resentment or anger. Next to their name, briefly write what they did to you.

As you think of each person, see if there is any of your power you lost to him or gave up as a result of that experience. Ask the person to return that piece to you. You may be able to identify the piece as your self-esteem, childhood, freedom, etc., or it may look like an object, or you may not see anything but just have a feeling that the person is giving you something. You may end up with one or two items, a basketful or a truckload.

If the person will not return the parts to you, have your inner guides or power animal help you retrieve them. They are working for you and have ways to get the parts back. Once you get the pieces back, put them in the fountain of light and clean them to your vibration and finish as we did in the reclaiming exercise above.

When you are whole and in your power, you may still experience—*but won't get stuck in*—conflict, depression, loss, or any of the other emotions that are upsetting to you. Check in with your feelings, and you will know when it is necessary to reclaim a part of yourself.

Logic Challenged

Although soul retrieval is not easily explained to the satisfaction of the logical mind, the results show it to be a successful method for clearing present-day health issues, mending broken hearts, improving relationships, dissolving blockages, dissipating fear, and restoring peace, self-confidence, clarity, and lightness to your being.

The reclaiming process can be used often for achieving wholeness and self-empowerment. Each time you do it, you experience a greater feeling of wholeness, even if you retrieve the same piece several times. This does not mean it didn't work the first time, it just means that you are now open and ready to accept more of its essence.

Fragmentation has been the accepted method through which humanity has chosen to learn, but the time has come to begin the integration process. Remember that you are whole within yourself and also part of the oneness. There are many different paths to take on this journey. One method that has proven to work quickly and easily in achieving wholeness is the process of reclaiming the lost parts of self, also known as soul retrieval.

Chapter 8
Letting Go

Anything you give your attention to will be-come your truth.

Esther and Jerry Hicks
Ask and It is Given

Filling the Space

Nature abhors a vacuum and the same is true with people. When you are not whole within yourself, you struggle to quickly fill the void. Since you just want things fixed, you are not always discerning about what is used to plug the hole. You may take on thought patterns, beliefs, addictions, judgments, attitudes, programs, negative emotions, or implants from parents, peers, teachers, church, medical establishment, television, etc.

You may also try to fill yourself by taking pieces from other people. I say "try" because filling yourself with another's energy doesn't work very well. It doesn't satisfy and the high you get in the moment doesn't last, so you have to keep taking more.

Any energy you take on that is not your own can be harmful despite the service it may provide, because these energies control, cause lack of discernment, keep you in victimhood, and drain your energy. They also prevent you from retrieving our own pieces because there is no longer room for them.

Reclaiming and Letting Go Work Together

When you carry energies that are not your own, you can attempt to reclaim your pieces but they can't come back into you if the hole has already been filled. In order to make room, you have to let go of clutter. Sometimes this will just happen as the piece comes in, but if it doesn't, you need to do a *releasement*[1] along with the reclamation. This clears the space and allows the piece to come back into its rightful place.

There are times when you have "lost" a piece of self and have not yet filled the space. If this is the case, you

---

[1] Releasement – An exercise to let go of attached energies that are not for your best and highest good. See the exercises at the end of this chapter.

need only retrieve the missing piece and return it to its rightful place because there is nothing there to prevent it from entering.

If you had a piece missing and filled that space with something else, you may have difficulty releasing that attachment. It has provided a feeling of security, false though it may be, and it is just too scary to think of feeling that emptiness again. This requires doing a retrieval and a releasement at the same time, so the lost part comes in as the attachment leaves.

Alicia had two pieces returned and cleared, but they would not go in. Her subtle bodies were filled with bitterness and self-righteousness and they would not open to the pieces. They said they would not allow them in because it would make her soft.

As the spiritual surgeons talked to the bodies, an attached energy came forward. She had agreed to its presence because life had been hard and she did not want to feel. Its job was to protect her by keeping her tough and numb.

Once removed, the two pieces flowed
easily into her. She was able to feel their
warmth spread through her body.

Programming

Some attachments are taken on eagerly and some come in the process of growing up. You accept many beliefs, patterns, thoughts, perceptions, judgments, traditions, and programs that are not your own in order to survive in everyday life. People and organizations are all vying for you to accept their programs. Your parents taught you to do your chores before you could go out and play. Teachers said if you talked or chewed gum, you would be sent to the principal's office. The boss said if you didn't do the job fast enough, you would be fired. In other words, if you did not do what was expected, horrible things would happen.

Following the rules may make living in our culture less confrontational, but to live life freely, you must recognize it as the programming it is. At the time, there may have been good reasons for the programs you accepted, but you need to determine if they are helping you today. Times change, ideas change, and maybe it is time to change the old programming that is no longer serving. Until you do, your life is controlled by fear of the consequences of non-compliance.

People are especially vulnerable to other's belief systems after experiencing hard times or a trauma that causes them to lose their power. Everything they believed was true before the event may now appear false. Everyone they thought loved them may now seem to have turned against them. There is a need to grab onto something or they feel they will be lost or annihilated. There must be something to believe in that can save them.

> Amy's mother died when she was an infant. She was placed in a children's home and grew up there. She never had the experience of having a mother or anyone else who lovingly cared for her.
>
> She searched to find her place in the world, going through some exceedingly hard times. She found a church where she was accepted. They took her in and she was born again. She accepted their teachings and was able to find stability in her life.

In times of chaos, people long for the security of concrete ideas and beliefs to give them stability. This helps them develop needed discipline. It gives them a way to fit in with a group. However, there may come a day when these beliefs are no longer appropriate, as they can hold us back and cause blockages. It takes wisdom to see when the time comes to let such things go and strength to change what no longer works.

Maybe you remember as a child being told that something you knew to be true was not correct. You figured you must be wrong because your parents, who knew everything, told you it was different from what you thought. If that happened a number of times, you may have quit thinking your own thoughts—it was just too confusing. You grew up accepting as real whatever you were told. This is the confused state the masses of people on this planet reside in today.

So many of these programs have accumulated that people get weighed down by the burden. It is a wonder they ever have an original thought. Perhaps they don't and that is why history keeps repeating itself.

Implants

In the broadest sense of the word, an implant is anything that has become a part of the energy field that surrounds your body that is not your own energy. These include thoughts, beliefs, attitudes, and programs, which have already been discussed. Some other types of implants are: needles, crystals, weapon energy, fog, programmed chips, sacred symbols or sounds, and various other devices.

You place many implants yourself, but some come from others—weapon energy, for instance. If you have been shot or attacked with a knife, you could still be carrying the energy of that weapon in your field.

Not feeling strong enough to survive on your own is one motivation to place an implant. Wanting excitement, *not* wanting to take responsibility, or the desire to learn something are other reasons. You may have implanted something to keep you safe, to keep you on track, or to have its energy work with you.

You could have implanted something to punish yourself. If you feel guilt or shame, you might put an energetic knife into your abdomen or heart and turn it every so often to remind you that you are a sinner. Such acts of martyrdom are not saintly, but destructive deeds of self-hatred and self-judgment.

Another destructive force in your field comes when someone blasts you with energy. If the person is filled with a powerful emotion and has to release it, he may direct it at someone else. For instance in child abuse, the anger that the adult carries is transferred down his arm and into the child as he strikes her. The child carries the anger, grows up, and can't understand why she is so angry. She thinks it is her own anger when really it is energy that belongs to the parent.

There are many other types of implants. Some are old and no longer used, while some are very active. Some served us at one time, but are now a hindrance in our lives.

Indications of Implants

It is not uncommon to have implants, thoughts, and programs attached. The following are just a few indicators that suggest the presence of this condition.

- Doing things and not remembering doing them, or not knowing why you did them.
- Wanting to move forward in life and not being able to.
- Feeling guilty, fearful, angry or powerless, oftentimes for no apparent reason.
- Having grown up in child abuse.
- Not being able to do things that are good for you.
- Wanting to do something and feeling blocked.

- Not wanting to do something, but feeling powerless to *stop* doing it.
- Being raised in an environment of not being able to speak or act outside severely strict rules.
- Saying things like, "That's not like me," "I don't know where that came from," or "People always walk all over me."

One of these things by itself is probably not enough to say that you are clinging to some attachment, but it is still something to consider.

Since you are the one who ultimately must claim responsibility for the thoughts you think and the deeds you do, it is important that you are the one in charge of your reality. If you have any of the indicators listed above, you may need to let go of something you are holding onto and reclaim a part of self.

Returning Pieces To Others

Once you have reclaimed your fragments, you can give back to others the power you have taken from them. This won't be difficult once you start coming into your own empowerment. In fact, you will find it cumbersome to drag around stuff that does not belong to you.

You can take an inventory of what you have that is not yours. Perhaps at work you take on more than your own responsibility, and find you are getting tired and burned out. Perhaps you put in long days and don't get to see much of your family. Perhaps you are the one everyone turns to when they have a problem. Maybe you are the one the PTA or the church group calls every time there is a job to be done.

Perhaps you are carrying responsibility for another person that is not yours to carry. Maybe you are a parent with grown children. All their young lives you protected them and kept them safe, but it is time to ask yourself if you can release them to live their lives, and yes, even make their own mistakes. This can be very hard to do. It is good to give service, but only when it is really yours to give. You must be clear about when, where, and how much to give.

As you reclaim your pieces, you grow stronger. You are then willing to give back pieces you have taken from others. When you let go of that which is not yours, you create room for more of your own pieces to return.

Exercise: Releasing Negative Energy

An easy technique you can use to clear old or harmful energies is to repeat the following affirmation. This is a simple exercise and takes very little time, yet is highly effective in creating clarity, balance, and peace of mind. Feel free to change, add or subtract anything to fit your situation. Say it three times, breathing out after each repetition. As you exhale, intend that you are releasing the attachment as well as any debris these things may have left within you. Allow the oxygen of your breath to flow through you so it can clean and clear your body.

> In the highest and best interest of myself and all that is, I now release, rescind, and break all agreements, contracts, commitments, oaths, pacts, vows, hexes, spells, past debts, research, ownerships, cords, or ties of any kind to any and all belief systems, thought structures, programs, judgments, implants, traditions, guilt, blame, anger, people, places, and things that are no longer serving me in the highest way. I do this throughout all time, in all dimensions, and in all bodies. And so it is.

It is important to say this affirmation with personal authority. Just rattling it off will have little effect. It is the power of your intention that causes it to work because it focuses your attention. You can repeat this affirmation every day, as you will be ready to release more each time you do it. Old programming sheds itself in layers.

If you find this does not totally clear the subtle bodies, ask the spiritual surgeons to help you remove anything that is no longer serving your highest good. You might also want to reclaim more of your pieces and then do the affirmation again. You can also work with the following "Letting Go" technique for further assistance.

Exercise: Letting Go

Usually letting the attached energies go is a simple process that you can easily do for yourself. The following exercise can be done in meditation, or when you get adept at it, standing in the shower.

Set up the space to work as we learned in Chapter 4.

Once you are ready to work, go into your fountain of light. Stand in the part of the fountain where liquid light is flowing down. Invite the light to stream over and through all of your bodies, the physical, supra-physical, emotional, memory, mental, unconscious, and spiritual. As the liquid light flows through you, release into it anything that is no longer serving your highest good.

Release stress, fear, pain, insecurities, anger, guilt, blame, and shame into the light. Let go of anything that is blocking you. Allow the light to do what is best with that which you release. What is not yours, the light will carry wherever it belongs. If it is yours and just not operating at the highest frequency, the light will clear and adjust it so that it can work in harmony with you. Allow and observe; there is nothing else you need do. The light knows what needs to be done and it will do the work if you allow it.

You can do this exercise along with the reclaiming exercise in Chapter 7. Do them as often as you like. Don't be afraid to release things that do not belong to you. As you claim your pieces, you won't need someone else's.

Alchemical Results

When reclaiming is combined with letting go, the clearing process truly becomes alchemical. As you do the work, it opens the way for others to do theirs, and as a result clearing occurs for everyone. Once you have retrieved your pieces and released what is not yours, the way to prevent it from happening again is to keep your subtle bodies clear and strong. You can do this by repeating the exercises in this book on a regular basis.

When the modern shaman reclaims what is his and let's go of what is not, the result is a gain of self-confidence and power, clearer boundaries, more balanced relationships, and greater peace and joy in life.

Chapter 9
In Closing

Over every mountain there is a path, although it may not be seen from the valley.

James Rogers

Completion

You are the creator of your life. Your thoughts and emotions are the tools you use to create. What you think and what you feel create what you see and experience every day. So it is important that you keep your thoughts focused on the things you want in life.

While it is true that fragmentation is only an illusion, we have to get to the place where we bring this highest truth into manifestation. As you read the information and worked through the exercises in this book, you used alchemical processes to get closer to this realization.

There are many ways to end the illusion of fragmentation and come into the awareness of your true self. Reclaiming your pieces and releasing what is not yours are tools I have found priceless in helping myself and others reach this goal.

The only limitation I have found with this work is the extent of our willingness to grow and change, as nothing will come that we are not able and willing to encounter. If you are wanting fuller expression and are willing to accept the changes this will bring into your life, there is no limit to what you can achieve using these processes. They can be repeated over and over, each time bringing back and releasing more.

As you open to more of your power, more will return. This allows you to feel safer about releasing that which you no longer need. Once you begin getting your pieces back and releasing those that are not yours, the knot of energy theft starts to unravel. This initiates a chain reaction, and clearing occurs for everyone.

This is the work of the modern shaman. Shamanism has been kept a secret in many tribes for many years. Today it is offered openly *to you*.

Exercise: Bringing the Curtain Down

As with any fine performance, you know it is over when the curtain comes down and the performers all take their final bow. The same is true with the clearing work. There is a closing that lets your body know the session is finished. It helps put things in order and makes sure that everything is aligned and working together so it all integrates with ease.

When I first began the clearing work, I always set the space, but I didn't pay as much attention to the closing until a client called and said that after the session she had pain in her arm. We had retrieved a piece of her arm and it was having trouble integrating. After that, I always included a closing statement of intent and no one since then has had difficulty with the integration.

You can use the following statement for the final integration, or you can create your own.

> I bring all my bodies and chakras together and ask that they align so they are all working in harmony. I stand in a column of light with any aspects that are ready to come back and ask that we all be brought to our highest potential. We merge in whatever way is perfect and right for me. Any other pieces that I am ready to get back I call into the fountain of light, ask that they be cleaned to my vi-

bration and come back into me in whatever way is right for me.

I release anything into the light that is
not serving my highest good. I bring a
golden light down through the top of my
head and ask that it integrate all the
pieces I have gotten back and the work
that has been done. I bring a golden light
into my abdominal area and let it spread
up to my head and down to my feet filling
my entire energy field, keeping me safe
and protected while this work integrates,
so that it is all done for my best and highest good and so that nothing can interfere
with it. And so it is.

I thank my divine self, teachers,
guides, spiritual surgeons, and anyone
else that worked with me.

This statement does several things. It aligns the bodies
and chakras so they are working together. It brings everything into alignment so integration is accomplished more
easily. It releases energies that couldn't previously be released. It sets up a protective field so all can integrate without interference. And it expresses gratitude for all that was
received.

Going through this list of intentions helps to smooth the energies so everything fits into your life with ease and grace, and without trauma or drama. By completing the work in this manner, it eliminates any problems with the parts returning.

If you are helping another person with the work, it is best to wash your hands when you have finished. It will help you break the connection with the other person. It becomes a signal to the bodies to relax and disconnect.

Walking the Path

I would like to close with the story of my friends Esther and Steven who have practiced the ways of the modern shaman. For Esther it began years ago when she set the intent to get in touch with her true self and to walk the spiritual path. Steven's journey to becoming a modern shaman took a little longer. This is the story Esther told to me.

> *Before I met my husband, I was journal writing every day. Instead of thinking, I listened. As I listened, I received information and knowledge about who I was and what I needed to do. My spiritual guidance told me I would not walk my life path alone—that a companion would walk*

with me. I was also told I would know him when we met.

Daily I listened to my spiritual guidance. I was led to a town where there was a group of people who were questioning religious programming and were starting to follow their spiritual guidance.

I went to a meeting and as I sat listening to the speaker tell his story, another man walked into the room and sat down close to me. I felt my guides walk in with him. One stood on my left and one on my right. There was a sweeping motion through my body. At that moment I remembered the promise that had been made to me.

"Ye shall feel the marrow in thy bones melting and ye shall know that truly this is the one of whom I speak."

That was my exact feeling when I looked at this man—I felt it in every cell of my body. I was consumed by it. I wept uncontrollably. The man thought I was reacting to the speaker's words. He felt the connection between us, but didn't understand how our lives were about to change.

Within six months, Steven and I were married. We lived in a small town in Kansas. Things in life were not working very well and Steven was frustrated and angry. I was trying to practice the things I had learned, but it often felt like I was on a roller coaster ride.

When guidance told us it was time to leave that area and move to another state, Steven realized that if life was going to change, he had to shift his thinking and become accountable for what life brought to him. He realized that financial worries had caused him to lose site of the miracles he had previously experienced.

As Steven thought back on how we met and other synchronicities we had shared, he made the decision that with the move, he would leave behind the anger and negative thinking. He made a conscious choice to become the creator of his life and to begin appreciating what we had. It was this change of thinking—in both of us—that lifted us into a new sphere of spiritual existence.

Last year, due to some health issues, I felt a need for emotional and physical clearing. My desire and intent to go deeper into my inner work brought Nancy De-Young into my life. She taught me the etheric clearing exercises. As I did them, my physical body actually felt the work. I knew deep inside that amazing healing was taking place. I felt an emotional strength I had not known before.

In the twelve years Steven and I have been together, our lives have been an incredible journey. Steven has gotten all the work he wanted, money has flowed, our health has improved, and our relationship has excelled. We are very happy and our lives keep getting better every day. We are walking our path—the path of the modern shaman.

Esther and Steven are an inspiration to those they meet. Because of their willingness to listen to and follow their spiritual guidance while taking full responsibility for their lives, they are now blessed in ways they could only imagine when they met.

Bringing change into your life may not always be easy, but the information and exercises in this book will help make the transition easier. You, and you alone, have the power to change anything you do not like about your life. You can do this by becoming a modern shaman. Your journey begins here and now.

Recommended Reading

Affirmations by Stuart Wilde, 2000, Hay House, Inc., Carlsbad, California.

Animal Speak by Ted Andrews, 1993, Llewellyn Publications, St Paul, MN.

Ask and It Is Given by Esther and Jerry Hicks, 2004, Hay House, Inc., Carlsbad, California.

Feelings Buried Alive Never Die by K. Kuhn Truman, 1991, Olympus Distributing Company, Las Vegas.

Heal Your Body by Louise Hay, 1988, Hay House, Inc., Santa Monica, California.

The Holographic Universe by Michael Talbot, 1991, HarperCollins Publishers, New York, New York.

Journal to the Self by Kathleen Adams, 1990, Warner Books, Inc., New York, New York.

Books by P.M.H. Atwater, L.H.D.

The Magical Language of Runes

Coming Back to Life: The Aftereffects of the Near-Death Experience

Beyond the Light: What Isn't Being Said About the Near-Death Experience

Future Memory: How Those Who 'See the Future' Shed New Light on the Workings of the Human Mind

Children of the New Millennium

Goddess Runes

As You Die (CD and DVD)

The Complete Idiot's Guide to Near-Death Experiences

The New Children and Near-Death Experiences

We Live Forever: The Real Truth About Death

Beyond the Indigo Children: The New Children and the Coming of the Fifth World. The addendum to the book, entitled "Beyond the Indigo Children EXTRAS" is on her website http://www.pmhatwater.com

The Secrets in My Soul (release in 2007)

The Near-Death Experience ~ A Single Sourcebook That Tells All (release in 2007)

Photograph by Gabrielle Nelson

Nancy DeYoung became interested in working with subtle energies as a result of her experiences in the Great Pyramid of Egypt. When she returned home, she learned about etheric clearing, Reiki, and using essential oils. She became a pioneer in combining the modernized techniques of soul retrieval and spirit releasement in her etheric clearing work. Nancy has traveled extensively throughout the world teaching and doing group and earth energy work. Many of the techniques in *Modern Shamans* have been developed as a result of her travels and workshops. Her work presently consists of writing and doing private sessions, workshops, and retreats.